MAURICE ASHLEY

The English Civil War

A CONCISE HISTORY

with 166 illustrations and 3 maps

THAMES AND HUDSON · LONDON

Printed in Great Britain by
Jarrold and Sons Limited, Norwich

ISBN 0 500 82002 3

CONTENTS

We have seen God marching so,
With our friends, against our foe,
As he did, long time ago,
  When his Isr'el was oppressed;
And, securing us from fear,
When our hopes at lowest were;
When despis'd, we did appear,
  And our peril most increased.

    – a Parliamentarian view of the war.

'Tis to preserve his Majesty,
  That we against him fight,
Nor are we ever beaten back,
  Because our cause is right;

'Tis for religion that we fight,
  And for the kingdom's good,
By robbing churches, plundering them,
  And shedding guiltless blood.

    – a Royalist view of the Parliamentarians.

PREFACE

In this book I have concentrated mainly on the causes of the English civil war and the course of the campaigns. I have deliberately limited my descriptions of the political background because it was so complicated and is therefore hard to summarize accurately. Even today specialist historians are still arguing about such questions as when an Independent was not an Independent and when a Presbyterian was not a Presbyterian. My discussion of the consequences of the civil war is necessarily summary, for that would really require an epitome of English history over the following hundred years or more.

My indebtedness on the political and social side to the writings of Professor A. M. Everitt, Dr Christopher Hill, Mrs Valerie Pearl, Professor Ivan Roots, Mr Conrad Russell, Professors Lawrence Stone, Hugh Trevor-Roper and David Underdown, as well as to those of my friend Dame Veronica Wedgwood OM, will be obvious to any reader familiar with the subject. In re-reading S. R. Gardiner's famous volumes, written some eighty years ago, I have been struck by the accuracy of his narrative and the excellence of his judgment. For military history I am grateful for the flood of light which has been poured out by Brigadier Peter Young and his friends in the 'Sealed Knot' as well as the persuasive narrative of Professor Austin Woolrych. Dr Ian Roy's book on the Royalist army and Patrick Morrah's life of Prince Rupert are eagerly awaited; they have both been kind enough to have talks with me on their subjects. I have also ventured in writing about the last two campaigns to adapt a few sentences from my book *Cromwell's Generals* which is now unfortunately out of print.

MAURICE ASHLEY

1 August 1974

England at the time of the civil war.

Chapter One

LONG-TERM CAUSES

Of all the mid-seventeenth-century revolutions in Europe the one that took place in England was the most complex and fascinating. It involved no fewer than three civil wars: the first was fought from 1642 to 1646; the second began early in 1648 and resulted in the trial by some of his own subjects of King Charles I, a traumatic event which was followed by his execution; and finally there was the premature attempt during 1649–51 by Charles's eldest surviving son to regain his father's throne with the aid of Irish Roman Catholics and Scottish Presbyterians, which collapsed completely after the destruction of his army at the battle of Worcester.

All this happened in three sparsely populated kingdoms. Though one speaks (correctly) of the English revolution and the English civil wars, one has to remember that, politically at least, two occurrences that led to the conflict in England were the vain attempt by Charles I to suppress in 1639 and 1640 risings by his Scottish subjects, compelling him after an interval of eleven years to recall an English Parliament to ask it for financial aid, and the Irish rebellion which broke out in the autumn of 1641, sparking off civil war through an unresolved argument about which side was to control the English armed forces recruited to suppress it. Thus rebellions in Scotland and Ireland gave rise to civil war in a country with a much larger population, where the members of the governing classes – 'the political nation' consisting of the monarch and his Court, the peerage and the leading landed classes – mostly knew each other and had much the same habits and spent the same kind of lives. It was the split down the middle that developed among these ruling classes which brought on the war. To begin with, at any rate, the mass of ordinary people was little affected by the row between their masters. As a contemporary wrote, 'They care not what government they live under so as they may plough and go to market.' Another noted somewhat differently that 'there were very few of the common people that cared much for either of the causes but they would have taken any side for pay and plunder'.

Should the English revolution be attributed mainly to an economic 'crisis' in society? During the sixteenth century important economic and social changes had been taking place. The price of food doubled between 1500 and 1550; by 1590 it had almost quadrupled; and in 1640 the price of food was about six times what it had been in 1500. The causes of the price inflation were various. The influx of silver from Central and South America to Spain in effect depreciated the value of money throughout Europe; a 'population explosion' occurred, increasing demand; and lastly, in England, the sales of Church and in particular monastic property following the Protestant Reformation in the reigns of King Henry VIII and his son Edward VI created a state of economic confusion which may well have reduced agricultural output. Wages did not keep up with the increase in prices and neither did rents that had been fixed over long periods of time through leasehold agreements. Thus a state of general unrest was created among landlords, their tenants and the small cottagers or landless labourers.

But by 1590 the difficulties brought about through inflation were almost over. 'Around the 1580s the land market began to boom . . . and boomed for the next half century' (J. H. Hexter). Rents started to catch up and even run ahead of prices. Landed incomes, whether derived from rents or from direct farming, rose considerably towards the end of the sixteenth century and the early part of the seventeenth. Landlords grew more cautious about granting long leases and as soon as leases fell in heavy fines were imposed for their renewal or rents were raised. Thus landed incomes grew rapidly after 1590 and an increase in agricultural profits, especially from sheep-farming, took place. The theory that no profits were made

from land by the smaller gentry in the years that preceded the out-break of the civil wars and that the only way in which the aristocracy and the gentry could acquire real wealth was by obtaining gifts and offices from the King is no longer generally accepted. No doubt some landlords got into financial difficulties owing to extravagance or incompetence, but the majority were better off and had gained from the boom. Nor was it only the upper classes who benefited: it is clear that the yeomen, both small freeholders and leaseholders, were also waxing richer. It has been suggested that merchants and industrialists (who formed less than 10 per cent of the community) did not enjoy the same rise in profits before the civil wars as the landed men did. But even if that were so, it was certainly not members of this class who became eager agents of rebellion. Their preference was for peace, for war merely interrupted the course of trade.

A great deal of elaborate statistical work has been done during the last thirty years or more aiming to show a decline in the financial, social and political strength of the aristocracy from which the rising gentry and yeomanry profited. It has been stated that the sixty peerage families which existed about 1540 had been obliged to sell off much of their land. 'There is overwhelming evidence', writes Professor Lawrence Stone, 'that the holdings of the surviving peers of 1558 [that is to say the forty peers who remained when Queen Elizabeth I came to the throne] had fallen by about a quarter by 1602 and by a further fifth by 1645.' Thus the average landholding by all peers declined by nearly a half as compared with the holdings of the same peers who existed in 1558. Their real incomes had fallen correspondingly. So, it is argued, there was 'a crisis in the aristocracy' owing partly to the static rents received by the nobility during the

Sheep-raising, upon which many fortunes of the time depended, is one of the occupations of the English countryside seen in this early seventeenth-century tapestry.

A carter and porter in a London street, drawn in 1614–15 by a visitor to the city, Michael van Meer.

years of the price inflation, partly to the need for them to indulge in conspicuous consumption in order to maintain their social status, and partly to incompetent management of their estates. No doubt, like the landed gentry as a whole, some peers 'fell' and some 'rose'. Yet several peerage families did exceedingly well, for example, out of sheep-farming; the Earl of Northumberland, the Earl of Devonshire, the second Earl of Salisbury, the Earl of Newcastle and the Earl of Worcester were all extremely wealthy men; so too in the first half of the seventeenth century were the Talbots, the Howards, the Spencers, the Montagus and others. An examination of the economic situation in eastern England in the Elizabethan and Jacobean periods has shown that there only the Crown and Church granted long leases. The fact is that the aristocracy, like the wealthier gentry, could 'stand a great deal of ruin'. Nor is it at all easy to distinguish between the aristocracy, the victims of this 'crisis', and the 'rising gentry' who are said to have grown in economic and political stature at its expense. Why should the younger sons or relatives of peers or the new peers created lavishly by King James I and King Charles I be differentiated from members of the ancient peerage, that is to say the peers who survived the reigns of Henry VIII and his children? Can one really isolate convincingly the economic classes that existed 350 years ago?

The fact is that no separation between rising peers and declining peers or between rising gentry and declining gentry offers any significant explanation of the long-term causes of the civil war. Some rich men were Royalists and some thriving gentry families were loyal to the Crown. Yet declining peers and declining gentry also sided with the King against Parliament. In the poorer parts of England and Wales the gentry, for the most part, fought for Charles I. Indeed the mixed farming (unenclosed, or 'champion') areas such as Kent, Norfolk and Suffolk were the most prosperous regions where the Parliamentarians were strongest, whereas in the mainly pastoral districts, such as Cheshire and Lancashire, the south-western shires and much of Wales, the inhabitants on the whole were loyal to the King. Thus the kingdom was better off than it had been for many years and it was not any economic crisis that led to the war. On the contrary, it was the growing prosperity of England, once inflation had come to an end, that made the gentry and lawyers who filled the House of Commons conscious of their claim to a much larger share in political power.

One important section of English society, however, did suffer from an economic or at any rate a financial crisis; that was the executive government of the kingdom, the monarchy itself. Queen Elizabeth I, despite her alleged parsimoniousness, had to sell property worth between £800,000 and £900,000, a lot of money for those days, just as Henry VIII had sold seven-eighths of the monastic lands which he appropriated, while in his son's reign most of the chantry lands were sold. James I, though pacific until towards the close of his reign, was grossly extravagant; so was Charles I, who had difficulty in raising resources to pay for his armies which he sent against the Spaniards and the French in 1626–27 and later the forces

Below left: Thomas Howard, Earl of Arundel, of Surrey and of Norfolk (*c.* 1585–1646). He increased his fortune by marrying the heiress of George Talbot, Earl of Shrewsbury, and became one of the greatest collectors of his age. Mytens painted him about 1618 with his famous classical sculptures, the first to be seen in England.

Below: a new country house in the latest fashion of about 1640, surrounded by its formal gardens and profitable lands, appears behind Hollar's elegant personification of Spring.

James I (1566–1625), a
portrait by Mytens of 1621.

Above right: Charles I (1600–
1649), painted by Van Dyck
about 1635.

Opposite
Above left: one of the Titians
bought by Charles I, sold by
the Commonwealth after his
execution.

Above right: Queen Henrietta
Maria's costume in Ben
Jonson's masque *Chloridia*,
designed by Inigo Jones in
1631.

*Below: An Allegory of Peace
and War* by Rubens. The
picture was presented to
Charles by the artist, who
had come to London as a
diplomatist in 1629 to
arrange a truce between
England and Spain.

which he led against the Scots in 1639 and 1640. He also spent
substantial sums on buying pictures and arranging masques to amuse
his wife. Between 1603 and 1613 James is estimated to have sold
land worth about £650,000, and between 1625 and 1635 Charles I
disposed of property worth about the same amount. The land
revenues of the Crown were estimated to have yielded less than
£10,000 a year on the eve of the dissolution of Parliament in 1629.
A wealthy peer or a merchant might have enjoyed a higher income
from his investments than that.

The consequence was that in order to pay for foreign wars
Charles I was driven to raise money by every conceivable means at
his disposal. Even after peace abroad had been obtained, since he
refused to allow Parliament to sit between 1629 and 1640, he levied
tonnage and poundage (that is to say duties on imports and exports)
without parliamentary permission and in face of much discontent
among the merchants who had to pay it, notably in the City of
London. The Customs were collected by 'farmers' who paid the
Government large sums of money in advance out of which they
earned a handsome profit. A test case (Bate's case) in the reign of
James I had conferred upon the Crown the prerogative right to
introduce new impositions as supplements to the existing Customs
duties. During the treasurership of Lord Portland, for example,

Mr. Alderman Abell and Richard Kilvert,
the two maine Projectors for Wine 1641.
From a very rare print in the Collection of R. P. Tighe, Esq?

'The two arrant Knights of the Grape', holders of the patent or monopoly on wine. Until Parliament put a stop to their activities in 1641, Alderman Abel (whose rebus, 'A bell', appears on the left) and his cousin Richard Kilvert levied a charge of 1d. a quart on French wine and 2d. a quart on Spanish wine.

new duties were levied upon coal and taxes on imported tobacco increased. The Exchequer judges upheld the King's right to collect the proceeds of these duties. In addition irritating feudal rights belonging to the Crown, which had fallen into disuse, were revived. Lord Portland was delighted by the idea of fining all gentlemen who owned land worth £40 or more a year if they refused to accept the dubious honour of knighthood. Patents, which their critics called 'monopolies', were granted, for example, for new ways of making soap and refining salt. Above all, Charles I's Government revived an Elizabethan tax known as 'ship money', which had been levied on seaports and coastal counties to pay towards the cost of the royal navy. In 1638 the tax was extended from the coastal areas of England to inland counties. It was a thoroughly economical tax, easy to collect, for the duty of doing so was given to the Justices of the Peace, who delivered the money to the sheriffs who then handed it over to the Admiralty. About £750,000 was raised by ship money during the years between 1637 and 1640 and it aroused intense indignation because everyone who had any means at all had to contribute. Although John Hampden, a wealthy Buckinghamshire squire, brought a test case over it, the judges held by a majority that the King was entitled to collect ship money if he considered that the kingdom was faced with dangers at sea (from pirates or otherwise) and that he alone was the judge of when such an emergency occurred. Thus because of his financial difficulties the King was compelled to demand money from his subjects in new and unpopular ways and it was widely considered that private property was in peril. 'What foolery is this,' remarked one gentleman, 'that the country in general shall be thus much taxed with great sums to maintain the King's titles and honours', that is to say as ruler of the Narrow Seas.

By the King.

A Proclamation for the levying and payment
of the Ship-Moneys in Arreare.

Hereas His Majestie, out of His Princely care of the defence of this Realm, and safety of His Subjects; Understanding of the great preparations of Shipping beyond the Seas, as well this present yeer, as in divers yeers preceding, and the imminent perils thereby appearing on every side to these dangerous and warlike times: For the speedie defence of His Kingdom and people, guarding of the Seas, and secure conduct of Shipping and Merchandize, (wherein all His Subjects were concerned) Did in divers yeers past, as in November last, direct His severall writs to severall Sheriffs, Majors, Baylifs, and other His Officers and Subjects, of the severall Counties of England and Wales; Thereby commanding the providing and getting in readinesse certain Ships furnished with Ordnance and Arms, and manned and victualled at the charges of the said Counties, in such sort as by the same writs were appointed. But His Majestie finding, that the said Ships were not provided according to the Tenour of the said writs, nor the moneys Levyed (according to Estimates yeerly given by the Lords, and others of His Majesties Privie Councell) for setting forth those Ships; His Majestie, for the common defence and safety of His Kingdom and people, was constrained at His own great charges, yeerly to make out, and maintain that Shipping which he expected from His Subjects.

And therefore His Majestie, as he cannot but censure the most of His Sheriffs and other his Ministers, of great neglects in the execution of that Service, according to their Oaths, and the duty of their places: So He will now expect from them an undelayed and faithfull performance of the same, without favour or connivence. And to that end, His Majestie doth hereby straitly charge and command, all His present Sheriffs, Majors, Baylifs, and other His Officers and Ministers to whom it appertaineth, forthwith not onely to raise and levie the said Moneys appointed to be collected and raised for the providing and furnishing the said Ships for this present yeer, But also to give forth their warrants to the preceding Sheriffs, Majors, and other Officers respectively, for the raising and levying of those Arreares which hapned in their times: And that as well the Sheriffs, Majors, and other Officers for this present yeer, as those for the yeers past, who are in Arreare to His Majestie, shall make their payments respectively, to the Treasurers of His Majesties Navie, at or before the first day of October next, without further respite or delay; upon pain of high contempt against His Majestie, and to be further proceeded with, and punished according to the quality of their offences, in that which so much importeth the publike good and safety of the Kingdom.

Given at the Court at Whitehall the twentieth day of August, in the sixteenth yeer of His Majesties Reign.

God save the King.

Imprinted at London by ROBERT BARKER, Printer to the Kings most Excellent Majestie: And by the Assignes of JOHN BILL. 1640.

Ship money. *Below:* an engraving of the ninety-gun warship the *Sovereign of the Seas*, built in 1637, which was published as propaganda for the tax. *Left:* an edict of Charles I in 1640 ordering the payment of all arrears. *Above:* John Hampden (1594–1643), who led the opposition to the levy (*see also* p. 40).

An examiner in one of the Church courts, from a pamphlet 'relating the fearfull abuses and exorbitancies of those spirituall Courts'. Styled as Sponge the Proctor, he is assisted by Hunter the Parator, who boasts that he 'had gotten good booty' from his office.

So deeply was ship money disliked that in the end many people refused or evaded its payment. Just as contemporary revolts against the Spanish Government were sparked off by the imposition of new taxes, so Charles I's financial difficulties, as well as his policies, stood first among the long-term causes of the civil war.

But another long-term cause was the animosity felt towards the leaders of the Church of England by the Puritans. Some historians no longer consider it correct to write of 'the Puritan rebellion', but unquestionably the Puritans played a major part in the coming of the civil wars. The Puritans, whose beliefs about the correct procedure and organization of church services were derived largely from the French theologian, John Calvin, had been crushed during the reign of Queen Elizabeth I. But James I, who came to England from Scotland, where the Lowlands were extremely puritanical, made a serious effort to reach agreement with their spokesmen.

The Puritans thought that preaching was more important than set prayers, that an individual believer could establish a direct contact with the Almighty without the intervention of Church or priest, that he could have been elected by God to 'salvation' from the beginning of time, and that all remnants of Roman Catholic ritual must be eliminated from church services. The researches of Dr Christopher Hill have shown us many of the economic grievances felt both by the Puritans and by others against the Church of England. They resented having to pay the various tithes, that is to say taxes which might amount to one-tenth of the harvest, in order to support the Church or to meet the demands of landowners who had bought these tithes for a capital sum (these were known as 'impropriations') from the Church; they disliked the Church courts which could impose humiliating punishments on members of congregations who were deemed to have sinned; they objected to fees and dues that had to be paid by law on the occasions of christening, marriage, funerals and so on; they resented paying for the upkeep of clergy who did not preach. No doubt all that was important, but even more significant were the sermons and exhortations of Puritan ministers or lecturers who managed to obtain access to pulpits and preached – by implication at least – in criticism of the Church hierarchy; and Charles I was after all the Supreme Governor of the Church.

Charles had in 1633 selected William Laud, who had been one of his chaplains and President of St John's College, Oxford (it was in Cambridge that the Puritan intellectuals flourished most), as Archbishop of Canterbury. Neither Laud nor his friend and patron, Richard Neile, who was to become Archbishop of York, belonged to the aristocracy. Laud was the tenth child of a Reading clothier and Neile reputedly the son of a man who made tallow candles. The austere King, who loved beautiful things and was the first Stuart to be brought up in the English Church, favoured orderly government and disliked the iconoclasm of the Puritans. Laud was

Opposite: William Laud, Archbishop of Canterbury, after the portrait painted by Van Dyck about 1636.

18

no theologian but he found predestinarianism distasteful. Therefore he tried, like one of his predecessors, Archbishop Whitgift, to sweep Puritanism out of the Church. But it was too powerful and he was too late. The Puritan preachers for the most part wanted to overthrow the Church establishment and to destroy the 'tyranny' of the new archbishops: this led to a movement to undermine the political establishment as well. Convinced and comfortable in the knowledge that they were God's Chosen People, their belief in themselves intensified their ardour to reform or recondition the Church. Most bishops thought that the Puritans were politically subversive. Parliamentarians, like John Pym and John Eliot, who were critical of the Government's policies, were not basically Puritans themselves. But the Puritans became their allies. It has been suggested that some Puritans came to believe that the King would never have been obliged to recall Parliament at all if 'the Saints' had not refused to pay their taxes. At any rate it was the intransigence of the Scottish Presbyterians, who were also King Charles's subjects, that compelled him to seek the aid of two Parliaments in 1640.

Thomas Hobbes (1588–1679) – *above*, a miniature by Samuel Cooper – and Richard Baxter (1615–91), *below*, who held that the Government had failed in its paramount duty to protect private property.

The theory that the first English civil war was a class war has never been abandoned by left-wing historians. If dubious statistical arguments no longer hold water, then contemporary literary evidence is relied upon as proof. We are reminded that the first Earl of Clarendon, who served both Charles I and Charles II, had insisted (in retrospect) that this was a war not about religion ('the Puritan rebellion', it has been claimed, was 'a nineteenth-century invention') but about property rights. Thomas Hobbes, the celebrated political philosopher, and Richard Baxter, a contemporary Puritan theologian, were both insisting that the first duty of government was to protect private property and because it failed to do so it provoked rebellion. James Harrington, another political theorist, thought the 'Gothic balance' had been upset through the acquisition of property by gentlemen, yeomen and merchants from the Church and the nobility and that the dissolution of society by such redistribution of wealth, which had begun in the reign of Elizabeth I, 'caused the war'. This analysis of a shift in the distribution of property seeks confirmation from other contemporary writers such as Thomas Wilson, who noted at the outset of the century that the gentry had improved their economic strength at the expense both of the Crown and the Church and of the smaller freeholders. An eighteenth-century historian, John Oldmixon, has even been dragged in for the opinion that 'a major part of the nobility and perhaps the gentry' sided with the King in the civil war, while nine out of ten of the merchants, clothiers and middling yeomanry all along supported Parliament. But this literary evidence is far from convincing. Serious work that is now being done on county histories shows that no clear-cut picture is to be found of class conflict. In most cases the gentry was divided; as to the merchants, it was to emerge that the big trading centres were by no means

Opposite: the Puritan view of the importance of the sermon, the 'immortal seed' that falls on fruitful (right) and barren ground, illustrated on the title-page of a book by Thomas Taylor, a Puritan minister at Reading.

21

'As the sun illuminates the world so does the King's return gladden the city.' A medal struck to commemorate Charles I's return to London after his coronation in Scotland in 1633 shows the city from across the river, dominated by St Paul's Cathedral and old London Bridge.

unanimously for Parliament. Many in London, Bristol and New-castle came to be committed Royalists. Furthermore it has been forcibly argued that in respect of economic interests no perceptible difference between peers, knights and gentlemen at Court and their counterparts in the country is to be discerned; thus even if a conflict did exist between Court and country it was not rooted in social and economic contradictions.

In any case is it right to job backwards from the character and economic status of the men who actually fought for and against the King when the war broke out in 1642 to the social and economic changes in an earlier period? The fact was that when Parliament was called in 1640 almost the entire House of Commons and many of the Lords were critical of the King's policies and administration, and legislation was forced through to prevent the monarchy from exploiting its prerogative rights to increase taxes. The future Earl of Clarendon himself was then among the critics of the monarchy. It is not until the end of 1641, when about half the members of the Commons came to the conclusion that the attack on the Crown had gone far enough, that the divisions between future Royalists and future Parliamentarians can be analysed; and an analysis that has been carried out has shown that no significant social, economic

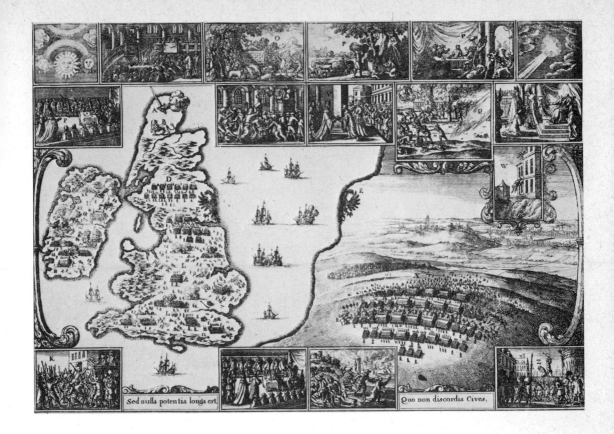

Sed nulla potentia longa est,

Quo non discordia Cives,

or financial differences existed between these two sides. This is not to the liking of proponents of class war, but at any rate so far as the membership of the Commons is concerned it is a fact. If any clear differences are to be discovered once the war began, they are to be found in geographical factors, as has already been suggested. But even then only a very few counties were overwhelmingly in favour of one side or the other.

One distinguished historian has insisted that the transfer of a section of the national income away from the Crown, some of the peerage and the bishops to the middle class of gentry, officials and lawyers in the sixteenth century caused a shift in 'the social balance' which helps to explain the civil war 'in depth'. Three long-term causes of the civil war are therefore to be found: a decline in the respect for the monarchy, the inability of the Church to comprehend the Puritans, and the 'crisis' in the affairs of the aristocracy. Another historian has bluntly written of 'the rise of the solid middle class of lesser landowning gentry on the ruins of the ancient aristocracy'. Thus the 'bourgeoisie', beloved of the Marxists, are let in, as it were, by the back door. The assertion is made that to ignore the 'pre-conditions' that cause revolutions to be possible is foolish and it has been claimed that 'the view that there must be a direct relationship

An etching after Hollar combines the events of the Thirty Years War with the troubles in Britain. The vignettes include the Edinburgh riot of 1637 against the new prayer book (to the right of Scotland; *see* p. 41), an imagined view of Henrietta Maria encouraging the King as he dissolves Parliament in 1640 (to the left of Scotland; *see* p. 45), and Charles attempting to arrest the five members of the House of Commons (bottom, left of centre; *see* p. 60). In three of the vignettes at the top Hollar represents the ideal condition of England in church and countryside.

between social structure and political institutions . . . is widely accepted today'.

No one will deny that members of the House of Commons in the reign of Elizabeth I, James I and Charles I were more influential and more critical of the Government than they had been under the early Tudors. But no member of the Commons in 1640 thought in terms of overthrowing the monarchy or even of reducing its rights, but merely of reforming it by persuading it to assuage grievances caused by a revival of feudal rights. Even to assert that loyalty to the Crown had diminished is doubtful since the revolutionaries were to claim that they were fighting for the King as well as Parliament. The conclusion is that if war followed, it came about accidentally and by surprise. The genesis of the revolution is therefore not to be discerned in any class struggle, not even in 'the loss of grip' by the aristocracy. The man who lost his grip was King Charles I. The long-term causes of the first English civil war were essentially political and religious – grievances over arbitrary taxation, complaints about the organization of the Church, demands for a larger role for Parliament. By the time the war broke out the nobility was divided and uncertain about its allegiance and so was the bulk of the landed gentry. On both sides idealism was to be found. Many still believed in the divine right of monarchy and thought that in the last resort the supreme duty of a subject was loyalty to the throne. On the opposite side men of stature considered that the monarchical Government had been arbitrary in its behaviour and had betrayed the Protestant Church. Therefore the King needed to be deprived of his evil counsellors and forced to rely upon the advice of Parliament.

Chapter Two

IMMEDIATE CAUSES

Whatever the long-term causes of the civil war may have amounted to, the sequence of events that immediately led to its outbreak is not difficult to depict. It began after the accession of King Charles I to the throne at the age of twenty-five in 1625. Though his homosexual father had broken down physically and mentally in the last year of his reign, in his earlier days he had shown himself to be a shrewd politician and even at the end he offered his son some wise warnings about the future. Charles, on the other hand, was reserved, lacked a sense of humour and gave the appearance of being proud and unyielding. It has well been said that he was 'serious-minded but not industrious'. He had the misfortune of inheriting from his father as his principal Minister George Villiers, Duke of Buckingham, a seductive favourite who was vain, arrogant and unscrupulous. Buckingham made himself extremely unpopular not merely because of his extravagances but because of an unrealistic foreign policy which involved England in wars against both Spain and France.

It was because of the war with Spain that the King demanded a large sum of money from the House of Commons, though he failed to specify what he wanted it for. Naturally enough he assumed that he would get what he thought was necessary since Parliament had urged that the war should be undertaken. The Commons suspiciously offered two subsidies (about £140,000 in the money of that time) and refused to allow royal officials to collect tonnage and poundage for more than one year. The reason for the limitation was that the leaders in the House, such as John Pym, a well-to-do landowner long haunted by the bogy of Popery, wanted specific grievances to be remedied by the King. They were convinced that favouritism was being shown by the Court to Roman Catholics, especially as Charles had just married a young Roman Catholic French princess, Henrietta Maria. So Charles in a huff dissolved his first Parliament without obtaining what he wanted from it.

When his second Parliament met in February 1626, in spite of the fact that Pym and other critics of the Court had been prevented

George Villiers, first Duke of Buckingham (1592–1628), portrayed about 1625 by Rubens – who found his 'caprice and arrogance' alarming. *Below:* a drawing made in Paris when the Duke attended the marriage by proxy of Charles and Henrietta Maria. *Right:* a sketch for a ceiling in York House, Buckingham's London mansion, showing him escorted upwards by Minerva and Mercury while Envy tries to pull him down.

from being elected (they had been appointed sheriffs, ineligible for membership of the Commons), Sir John Eliot, a Cornish squire and a former friend of the Duke of Buckingham, took over the leadership of the House, condemned the complete failure of an amphibious attack on Spain organized by Buckingham during the previous year, and attempted to impeach him on the somewhat obscure charge of breaching 'the fundamental laws of England'. The King retorted by ordering Eliot's arrest and later dissolved Parliament. In a speech to both Houses Charles had reminded his audience that it was his right alone to summon parliaments and that if they misbehaved he would not do so. Charles's inability to extract a grant of money resulted in the imposition of forced loans on landowners and the billeting of troops on civilians. Despite such expedients the King never had the resources to make war upon another nation, let alone two. The attempt led by Buckingham in person to occupy the island of Rhé near La Rochelle, where French Protestant rebels were holding out against the Government of Cardinal Richelieu, was entirely unsuccessful during the campaigning season of 1627. In the same year five knights were arrested and imprisoned for their failure to pay the forced loan, the King refusing to show any cause for his action. Thus when, in order to obtain a money vote, Charles

called a third Parliament in March 1628 the Commons, filled with
landed gentry, were seething with grievances against the royal
Government.

The House of Commons of 1628–29, now again led by Pym and
Eliot, once more refused the King supplies until its various complaints – forced loans, compulsory billeting, arbitrary imprisonment
and the imposition of martial law – had been dealt with. A 'Petition
of Right' embodying these grievances was drawn up with the
approval of both Houses of Parliament and reluctantly accepted by
the King. Not satisfied with that, the Commons also condemned the
illegal collection of tonnage and poundage and again tried to
impeach Buckingham. On 26 June 1628 Charles prorogued Parliament after reminding it that he owed no account of his actions
except to God and that he scorned to threaten anyone but his equals.

During the adjournment Buckingham was assassinated by a
fanatic, but when Parliament met again in January 1629 its mood was
unaltered. In fact it was now obvious that the King's Ministers were

John Felton (c. 1595–1628),
who assassinated the Duke of
Buckingham in 1628. He
had served in Buckingham's
ventures in France and Spain,
and had personal as well as
political grievances against
him.

Left: Buckingham's
expedition to help the
Huguenots ended disastrously
on 8 November 1627, when
the French raised the English
siege of the island of Rhé.
The young Louis XIII
(Charles I's brother-in-law)
is shown on horseback in the
left foreground surveying the
operation.

27

no longer under attack but that Charles's own actions had become the implicit subject of criticisms. These criticisms were twofold: the first related to illegal taxation, the second to the religious policy pursued by the King in his capacity of Supreme Governor of the Church. In spite of a somewhat ambiguous statement in his prorogation speech Charles had continued to permit the levy of tonnage and poundage. As to religion, the Commons condemned 'the growth of Popery' both in England and in Scotland and the encouragement given to 'the Arminian sect', that is to say those churchmen who believed in God's universal grace and the freewill of all men to gain salvation. As has recently been stressed, by the 1620s the Church of England had been Calvinist theologically for approximately sixty years, accepting predestination, the doctrine which maintained that from the beginning of time some men are chosen to be saved and the rest are destined for damnation. However, the bishops appointed by Charles I rejected this terrifying dogma. When Buckingham became Chancellor of Cambridge University in 1626 predestinarian teaching had been forbidden, while at the end of 1628 the King in reissuing the Thirty-Nine Articles originally

Opposite: propaganda to feed anti-Catholic feeling. Published in 1627, this print recalls 'Popish plots and treasons' from 1569 (*1*) to 1605 (*16*, the Gunpowder Plot). The sequels appear at the sides, while at the bottom the 'True Church' tramples on the Devil, a monk and the Pope.

A Puritan satire shows 'Rattle-Head', compounded of Laud and the Queen's Jesuit confessor, rejecting a book offered by the Puritan, 'Sound-Head', and turning instead to the monk – the true 'Round-Head', according to the Puritans.

drawn up in the reign of Elizabeth I ordered that all 'curious research be laid aside'. The Thirty-Nine Articles could in fact be interpreted as both rejecting and accepting predestination, but for the most part the Elizabethan Church had accepted it. Therefore its rejection was genuinely regarded in the House of Commons as a Popish and Arminian 'innovation' poisoning the true waters of the Christian faith. The King was asked to uphold the 'orthodox doctrine' of the Church and to have the books of the innovators burnt, while the Puritans ruminated on a fresh grievance against the Church hierarchy.

It was over these two questions, the levying of tonnage and poundage and the innovations in religion, that the clash between the King and his Parliament took place in March 1629. In spite of the protest by the Commons Charles had defiantly appointed Arminians to bishoprics, chaplaincies and livings in his gift. When the Speaker of the House of Commons, acting on the King's orders, tried to adjourn it, he was held down in the chair while three resolutions proposed by Sir John Eliot were unanimously passed: the first condemned religious innovations, stating that anyone who introduced them was 'a capital enemy' to the kingdom; the second asserted that anyone who advised the levying of tonnage and poundage without the approval of Parliament was a capital enemy; the third stated that any merchant who voluntarily paid these duties was 'a betrayer of the liberties of England'. The House of Commons then broke up; another one was not to meet for eleven years.

Before turning to the startling events that occurred when Parliament met again in 1640 and to the reasons why the King was obliged to summon it, let us consider the political atmosphere that prevailed during the first fifteen years of Charles's reign. Recently much research has been done by American historians on the composition and character of early seventeenth-century parliaments, based largely on diaries kept by members. It is often said that the formation of an opposition to the monarchy can be traced back to the reign of Elizabeth I and that this opposition increased in the House of Commons during the 1620s. Sometimes the term 'revolutionists' is actually applied to the leaders of this opposition. Yet it is an anachronistic view. Admittedly the House of Lords was less powerful than it had been before and the right of the Commons to petition about grievances and to vote taxes had been fully established. Yet the attitude of the first three Parliaments of Charles's reign reflected not organized opposition but a general dissatisfaction with his government. The Petition of Right was passed unanimously as were also the three resolutions moved while the Speaker was held down in his chair in March 1629. Men who subsequently emerged as convinced Royalists – such as Sir John Culpeper and Sir Edward Hyde (the future Earl of Clarendon) – concurred in the general disapproval of the royal administration. Though even John Pym

Sir John Eliot (1592–1632), one of the leading opponents of religious innovations and the imposition of taxes without parliamentary consent. Charles I blamed his speeches for the assassination of Buckingham, and he died in the Tower.

gave lip-service to the Divine Right of Kings, respect for the monarchy was unquestionably upon the wane. Whatever faults King James I may have possessed, he never levied taxes without parliamentary consent nor did he have members of parliament arrested without showing cause. Who was this young man of twenty-five to treat his subjects with contempt? What right had he to plunge his country into the two wars incompetently managed by the Duke of Buckingham? Why should the goods of merchants be taxed and impounded without the consent of the Commons? Was the King not defying the constitution? The general attitude was not revolutionary but conservative. Men looked back with pride to the good old days of Queen Bess. They thought that they were being confronted with innovations in the State as well as in the Church.

But the political life of the kingdom was not concentrated solely in the House of Commons. It is in the counties, where the real work of government was carried on year by year at the assizes, in the magistrates' courts, at petty and quarter sessions with the aid of information given out from parish pulpits, that one can see how the discontent over the acts of the administration was growing. Naturally the character of the discontent varied somewhat from county to county; the political history of the counties has not yet been completely covered. But take Somerset, for example, which has recently been subjected to expert examination. Here local government was, as in practically all counties, in the hands of half a dozen gentry families. These gentry representing the county were antagonized by the extravagance and misgovernment of the upstart Buckingham. But the middling sort of the people, that is yeomen and tradesmen, also disliked the arbitrary taxes being imposed and the impressment and quartering of soldiers. It was among the county folk too that Puritan unrest with the Church hierarchy was strongest. Even Sir Ralph Hopton, who was later to be one of the ablest of Royalist generals, was a Puritan suspicious of Popery and opposed to forced loans and the regular levying of ship money. The conclusion is that the county was united against the Court as it had never been before. In Kent too a united opposition of a conservative character to the Government's policies existed in the 1620s. The gentry families were prominent in objecting to ship money. Men like Sir Roger Twysden and Sir Edward Dering, who were cousins and were to fight each other in the county election of 1640, were later both to become Royalists, yet before the war they were critical of the autocracy of the King's servants from Buckingham to Strafford and thought that Archbishop Laud was a dangerous innovator. Here again the county gradually united between 1630 and 1640 against the 'Arminians', against ship-money levies, and in favour of the recall of Parliament. In Yorkshire the gentry resented not only ship money but having to pay for the King's abortive wars against his Scottish subjects; yet when the civil war began there were twice as many active Royalists as active Parliamentarians in the county. As a final example, Cornwall, which was to prove the most Royalist of all counties during the civil war and the last to surrender to the Parliamentarian armies, was also united in its grievances over forced loans, ship money and religious innovations. The forty-four members of parliament for Cornwall, led by Bevil Grenville, who like Edward Hyde (another Cornishman) and Hopton, was a future Royalist, formed a homogeneous party allergic to the King's arbitrary measures.

If one turns from political to purely religious complaints one can again note that no Puritan 'party' or formed opposition to the Church existed. Those extreme Puritans who were actually prepared to separate themselves from the Church, the kind of men who sailed to settle in North America, were comparatively few in number.

Opposite: a song-sheet lamenting the excise on liquor.

32

The good Fellowes Complaint:

Who being much grieved strong Licqour should
In paying a Farthing a Pot for Excise.

To the Tune of.   Reged and torne and true.

Ome hither my jovall Blades,
and listen unto my Song,
us that of severall Trades,
have borne the burthen long :
so long as the Patentees,
sit long and kept on foot,
une knaves got by there feete,
the Devill and all to boote :
    ..fie upon this Excise,
        that ever 'twas paid,
    ..od Licqour to rise,
    ..is downe many a Trade.

    ..it first began,
    ..to crosse the Seas,
    ..English man,
    ..en the same disease :
    ..got it at first,
    ..then to maintaine,
    ..an old Duch woman nurst,
    ..'t in the Cradle of Spaine,
    ..n this Excise,
        t first was paid,   165
    ..od Licqour to rise,
    ..s downe many a Trade.

    ..Companion for Warre,
    ..ls a whole kingdome with care,
    ..owes where ever they are,
    ..ar a great part for their share:
    ..never should grieve me much,
    ..yough more Excises were,

The thing I onely grutch,
    is that of Ale and Beere :
I never would vex nor pine,
    what ever you say or thinke,
To dubble the price of Wine,
    for that I seld me drinke. But fie, &c

How ever it came to passe,
    that drinke is growne so dears,
The Tradesman is the Asse,
    which must the burthen beare,
What though the Brewer pay,
    mine Hoast payes him againe,
Whilst that good Fellowes they,
    do all the losse sustaine :
O fie upon this Excise,
    that ever it first was paid,
It makes good Licqour to rise,
    and pull downe many a Trade.

The Blacksmith which doth get,
    his living through the fire,
And being throughly het,
    to drinke heel' then desire,
He calls to another man,
    with him to spend his groat,
For 't was not a peny can,
    could squench the sparke in's throat
Oh fie upon this Excise,
    'tis pitty that ever 'twas paid,
It makes good Licqour to rise,
    and pulls downe many a Trade.

The most extreme opponents of the Church of England in the 1620s and 30s fled to the Lowlands and thence to North America, where they established Puritan colonies such as Plymouth in Massachusetts.

So were the avowed Presbyterians who wanted to abolish bishops and substitute a form of government similar to that of the Scottish Kirk. The Puritan movement flourished inside, not outside, the Anglican Church. Many Christians throughout England regarded themselves as intensely conservative. They wanted preaching to become a more central part of the Church services, they wished to pray to God after their own fashion, and they required the communion service to be purely commemorative. Above all, they honestly feared that the King with his Roman Catholic wife and his Catholic Ministers, such as the Lord Treasurer Portland and the Chancellor of the Exchequer Francis Cottington, was conniving at the Catholicization of the English Church. Edward Hyde was to write that 'the imputation raised by Parliament upon the King of an intention to bring in Popery . . . did make a deep impression on the people generally.' Many of the diaries and memoirs of gentry who were to emerge as Royalists – such as for example that of Dr Samuel Ward, the introspective Master of Sidney Sussex College, Cambridge – exemplify what may be called the Puritan habit of mind. They reveal a deep consciousness of sin and a conviction of belonging to the Elect, of intimacy with the Maker. Though some Puritans were more active than others, notably those who, like Oliver Cromwell, the squire of Ely, subscribed to the payment of lecturers – that is to say preachers who composed their own sermons and did not read them from prescribed books – the fact remains that by and large the bulk of the kingdom was critical of the existing ecclesiastical authority. In the House of Commons condemnation of

Charles I's bishops who paid visitations throughout their sees to ensure ritualistic conformity was virtually unanimous.

The King thought it right to publish a long declaration to his people as a whole after he dissolved Parliament on 10 March 1629. Though he began by saying that 'princes are not bound to give account of their actions but to God alone' he defended in detail his domestic and religious policies. He justified the continued levying of tonnage and poundage without parliamentary consent by appealing to precedents from the reign of Edward IV and he insisted on his care for religion, stating that he would never 'give way to the authorizing of anything, whereby any innovation may steal or creep into the Church' but would preserve the unity of doctrine and discipline established in the time of Queen Elizabeth I. Thus the King as well as the Commons claimed to be conservative.

The day after Parliament adjourned in 1629 Sir John Eliot and eight other members of the House of Commons were summoned to appear before the Privy Council and on the following day were placed under arrest for conspiring sedition. All but three were eventually released on making their peace with the King, but the Court of King's Bench decided that Eliot and two others were guilty of a crime and could be kept in prison at the monarch's pleasure. It is said that Charles felt bitterly towards Eliot on the ground that his speeches in the Commons had incited the assassination of the Duke of Buckingham. Three years later Eliot was to die unhappily in the Tower of London. The harsh treatment of Eliot exacerbated the feelings of former Parliamentarians against Charles I.

The King managed to govern without Parliament because he reduced his expenses and increased his revenues. Peace was concluded with both France and Spain. The yield from Customs rose, reaching an average of £400,000 a year between 1636 and 1641; ship money was levied from both ports and inland towns and realized about £180,000 during the first year. The King also revived various feudal dues including fines on those who had encroached on the royal forests and those who created depopulation by enclosures of common land. Money could be borrowed fairly easily from the City of London. Financially therefore the Government kept its head above water. Altogether the King had about a million pounds a year at his disposal. His son was only to be voted £1,200,000 a year by a loyal Parliament.

It has been contended by apologists for Charles I that he adopted a paternalistic policy towards the poor, who were better off than if the House of Commons had been sitting. A Book of Orders was issued to make local government more effective, poor rates were reinforced by commissioners and efforts were exerted to find occupation for the unemployed. Roads and canals were built, fens were drained with the assistance of Dutch engineers and a postal service was established. But as has justly been observed, 'the way that government worked in the early seventeenth century meant

Charles I, Henrietta Maria and their infant son Prince Charles, at table in about 1632. The setting of Houckgeest's picture, painted for Charles, is imaginary, and glorifies the royal family even more than their existing palaces could have done.

Opposite: a lesson in observing the Sabbath. On the left are the 'works of light' and on the right the 'works of darkness', among which the Puritans included the entertainments permitted by the reissued Book of Sports.

that State intervention usually led to good profits for some individual or privileged group, paid for by giving the King his share' – as, for instance, in the fenland draining schemes. It is doubtful if any consistent domestic policy was followed. In any case Charles did not neglect his own comforts, notably his hobby of collecting pictures.

In religion the King continued to favour the so-called 'Arminians'. Laud gave instructions that in the churches in his diocese the altars were to be restored to the east end of the nave and approved of the reissue of the Book of Sports which allowed amusements after services on Sundays, both moves calculated to offend the strict Puritans. Those who by word or deed repudiated the attempt to achieve religious uniformity were hauled before the Court of Star Chamber – a prerogative court – and could be punished severely. Laud had his good points. Unlike the King, he genuinely believed in promoting a social policy favourable to the poor and he aimed to ensure the beauty of holiness by maintaining a standard of decency and order in parish churches. Thus he approved of the wearing of vestments by clergy and of the congregations bowing towards the altar. In 1633 before becoming Archbishop of Canterbury he accompanied Charles to Scotland where the King was crowned in

Opera Lucis.

Opera tenebrarum.

DIES
DOMINICA.

Ignat. Ep. ad Magnes.

Μετὰ τὸ Σαββατίσαι,
ἑορταζέτω πᾶς φιλόχριστος
τ κυριακὴν, τ ὀναςσιμον, τ
βασιλίδα, τὴ ὑπάτην πασῶν
τ ἡμερῶν.

Post Sabbatum omnis Christi amator Dominicum celebret diem, resurrectioni consecratum Dominicæ, reginam & principem omnium dierum.

The ampulla used to contain holy oil with which Charles I was anointed at his coronation in Edinburgh, in June 1633.

Holyrood Palace. Because the Archbishop of Glasgow refused to wear a surplice at the ceremony, he was not allowed to take part in it. This visit alienated leading Lowland Scotsmen who hated both foreigners and Popery.

In that year too Laud's friend Thomas Wentworth was sent by the King to govern Ireland. Wentworth had earlier been highly critical of the monarchy and prominent in securing the passage of the Petition of Right through Parliament. But since the Petition had been accepted Wentworth entered the royal service and was created Viscount Strafford. After four years' work as Lord President of the

The Queen's Chapel in St James's Palace, begun by Inigo Jones in 1623 for Charles's intended bride, the Infanta of Spain, and completed in 1627 for his Roman Catholic Queen, Henrietta Maria.

North he was promoted to be Lord Deputy of Ireland where he carried out a programme of thorough political and economic reform, but did not omit to fill his own pockets. Charles's attitude to Wentworth was always cool, partly no doubt because of his past behaviour and partly because of his arrogance. Laud, who was twenty years older than Wentworth, the King trusted, even if he did not always follow his advice. In fact a principal royal counsellor was the Roman Catholic Queen who gave birth to three sons and four daughters and to whom Charles became devoted. He was once heard to say to her: 'I wish that we could always be together, and that you could accompany me to the Council.' Though that was not thought permissible, Henrietta Maria exerted her influence behind the scenes. As a Bourbon and a Medici, she was no lover of parliaments.

With Charles's revenues improving sufficiently for him to manage comfortably as long as his two kingdoms remained at peace, he might have been able to govern indefinitely without calling another Parliament. But in 1638 two events occurred which altered the

Charles I and Henrietta Maria with their first child, the future Charles II, born in 1630. The picture, painted probably in 1632 by the visiting Dutch artist Pot, celebrates their marriage as the union of war and peace; sprigs of olive and laurel symbolize the peace-making activities of James I and the military exploits of the Queen's father, Henry IV of France.

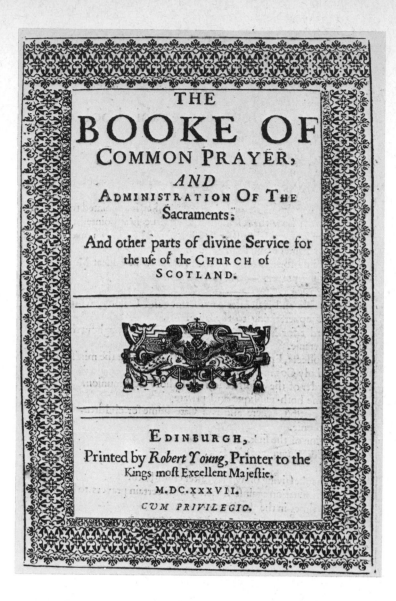

THE
BOOKE OF
COMMON PRAYER,
AND
ADMINISTRATION OF THE
Sacraments:

And other parts of divine Service for
the use of the CHURCH of
SCOTLAND.

EDINBURGH,
Printed by *Robert Young*, Printer to the
Kings most Excellent Majestie.
M.DC.XXXVII.
CVM PRIVILEGIO.

Title-page of the service
book which Charles I tried
to impose on the Scottish
Kirk in 1637.

entire situation. The first was the divided verdict of the twelve
judges in the test case brought by John Hampden about the legality
of ship money. This case focused the nation-wide dissatisfaction over
the levy of the tax upon all English counties during an era of peace.
The propaganda arising in consequence of the trial and the fact that
only seven of the twelve judges found in favour of the King brought
about a general refusal to pay the tax. Attempts to confiscate
property where the tax was refused resulted in the murder of one
official and intense indignation among the poorer farmers, whose
only cows were seized when they failed to meet their share of this
taxation. The second event was the King's decision to impose a
prayer book or liturgy formulated in London upon the Scottish

Kirk, which resulted in riots in Edinburgh, the drawing up of a National Covenant expressing the solidarity of the Scottish Lowlanders against English interference with their religious way of life, and the consequent resolve of Charles I that summer to prepare to enforce his will on his Scottish subjects by war.

The Church or Kirk had existed ever since 1567, the year in which Mary Queen of Scots had abdicated. Its doctrine was based on an extreme Calvinist position, embodied in a Confession of Faith, while the ecclesiastical organization in Scotland derived from a Book of Discipline which, unlike the Confession of Faith, had not been registered by the Scottish Parliament. In this reformed Kirk ministers were elected by their own congregations and discipline was entrusted to lay elders. Moreover the Kirk had been given the right by King James VI, when he succeeded his mother, to call General Assemblies which dealt with matters of religion and discipline. King James, however, believed that the Presbyterian system undermined the monarchy and he managed in 1600 to appoint four bishops to the Kirk, though – partly because they had no ecclesiastical courts – they did not possess the disciplinary powers that English bishops enjoyed. Charles I was determined that uniformity of religion should prevail in his two kingdoms. Little did he realize the resentment that the new prayer book would arouse. 'What he was doing,' as Gardiner remarked, 'he did from a love of order, combined with sheer ignorance of mankind.' But this resentment was not created solely by his attempt to insist upon the use of the new prayer book at Easter 1637. The Scottish nobility were at one with the leaders of the Kirk in resisting the claims of the bishops both in Church and State. They were united in opposing a new régime, of which this liturgy was the symbol, being foisted upon their ancient kingdom.

In February 1638 Charles was personally warned by his Lord Treasurer in Scotland that if he wished the new prayer book to be

The riot in St Giles's Cathedral, Edinburgh, when the Bishop of St Andrews attempted to read the new service book.

James Hamilton, Marquis and later first Duke of Hamilton (1606–49), Commissioner in Scotland for the King and like him a keen collector of works of art. Detail of a portrait by Mytens.

used he would have to support it with 40,000 men in arms. In that very same month the Covenanters were celebrating 'the great marriage day of the nation with God'. From then on Charles played for time to achieve his ends. He realized that he could not possibly be ready for war before the spring of 1639. Therefore he told the Marquis of Hamilton, whom he had appointed as his Commissioner in Scotland, to allow the use of the prayer book to be suspended and to permit a General Assembly of the Kirk to be called. The Assembly, which met in Glasgow instead of Edinburgh, because Hamilton believed that his own influence was stronger there, proved unreceptive to blandishments and grew defiant. When Hamilton ordered its dissolution it refused to obey and after rejecting the new prayer book it abolished the bishops. Both sides prepared for war.

This civil war between Charles and his Scottish subjects was not fought over the question for which the King had first contended. What in fact happened was that the King had provoked a Scottish national movement against him led by Presbyterian ministers who induced the canny citizens of Edinburgh to unloose their purse-strings. Everything was organized with typical Scottish efficiency. Professional officers, who had returned from fighting in the Thirty Years War in Germany, trained the stout young ploughmen in the military arts. Though none of the Highland chieftains (most of whom were Roman Catholic) took part in the war except for the saturnine and dedicated Marquis of Argyll and his Campbells, the

Marquis of Argyll

Archibald Campbell,
Marquis of Argyll (1607–61),
the only Highland chieftain
to fight against the King.

Lowlanders flocked to the colours. The King, on the other hand, lacked the funds with which to buy sufficient arms and supplies (for his revenues had contracted since the Hampden trial), while the militiamen from southern England who formed the bulk of his infantry had not their hearts in the northern war. Charles did however possess a small but splendid force of cavalry under the command of Lord Holland which crossed the border from Berwick on Tweed on Whit Monday 1639. But the mounted English soldiers recoiled before the vast lines of Scottish infantry. All Charles's advisers begged him to conclude peace. So he decided to abandon the campaign in the hope that the Scots would be divided in their allegiance and that he himself could raise a better army. By the Pacification of Berwick it was arranged that both armies should disband and that a Scottish Parliament and General Assembly should meet that autumn when the King himself would come to Edinburgh to complete a settlement.

The King never went to Edinburgh. On the contrary he regarded the agreement at Berwick as a mere truce. He thought that he had been unlucky in his first Scottish campaign. He had chosen the wrong commanders; he had failed to collect sufficient money; he had given in too soon: after all, the Scots had not actually fought against him. Therefore in the summer of 1639 he decided to send for his most successful servant, Viscount Strafford, his Lord Deputy in Ireland, to seek his advice and help. In fact Strafford had not approved of the Scottish war, not that he thought the King was wrong to assert his authority but because he considered that the whole operation was insufficiently prepared. Soon after Strafford arrived in London he combined with the Marquis of Hamilton and Archbishop Laud in pressing the King to summon a new Parliament at Westminster in order that he might obtain from it adequate supplies to wage war on the Scots. Surely loyal and patriotic Englishmen would rally to his assistance against their traditional enemies? Charles was always volatile. Strafford promised him money and troops from Ireland; the King hoped to raise a large loan in the City of London which had recently appointed a friendly Lord Mayor; he ordered the fortifications of Berwick on Tweed and Carlisle which guarded the main routes into Scotland to be strengthened and organized the manufacture of weapons of war in English arsenals. He showed his confidence in Strafford by raising him to the post of Lord Lieutenant of Ireland and granting him the earldom after which he hankered. Moreover he accepted the advice he gave to call a Parliament in England. While the arrangements for its election were being undertaken, Strafford returned to Ireland to collect subsidies and soldiers for his King.

Strafford had been so successful in manipulating the Irish Parliament that he was confident that a carefully worded appeal to an English Parliament would arouse a ready and loyal response. After all, Sir John Eliot was dead, John Pym was ageing, the English never liked the Scots. Strafford himself had been a leading member of the House of Commons and thought that he knew how it could be managed. But he was living in a dream world.

As has been noticed, during the eleven years' intermission between Parliaments grievances had accumulated in the English counties and boroughs where members were chosen. It is possible that both the royal officials and the critics of the Government, who were grouped round the wealthy Earl of Warwick (Pym had been the Secretary of the Providence Company of which Warwick and John Hampden were shareholders), tried to do what they could to influence the elections. But it is more likely that, as usual, the country gentry agreed among themselves about who the members should be, while provision was made for a few royal officials to be chosen, such as Sir Henry Vane the Elder, who had recently been appointed Secretary of State. But the atmosphere of the time was all against the Court. A rhymester who wrote

Robert Rich, Earl of Warwick (1587–1658). Leader of the critics of the Royal Government in the House of Lords before the war, he commanded the Parliamentarian navy and his son married one of Cromwell's daughters.

> Choose no ship sheriff or court atheist
> No fen drainer nor church papist

probably reflected the current prejudices. At any rate when Parliament met at Westminster on 13 April and was asked by the Lord Keeper for a generous supply of funds as well as the legalization of tonnage and poundage so that the King might win a victory over the rebellious Scots, Pym demanded in a two-hour speech that the

Thomas Wentworth, Earl of Strafford (1593–1641), Lord Lieutenant of Ireland and one of the King's principal advisers in 1639–40. Feared by the House of Commons, he was executed after the passing of an Act of Attainder in 1641. More than ten years earlier he had prophesied: 'Whoever ravels forth into questions the right of a king and of a people shall never be able to wrap them up again into the comeliness and order he found them.'

liberties and privileges of Parliament should first be attended to and the verdict given in the ship-money case be re-examined. Charles I offered to abandon ship money – which he was in fact no longer able to collect, so widespread was the discontent with it – if the Commons would vote him twelve subsidies (about £840,000). When after three weeks this offer was refused, the King dissolved what was to be known as the 'Short Parliament'.

The Earl of Strafford, who returned to London after a whirlwind visit to Ireland, did not approve of the decision to dissolve this Parliament; nor did Archbishop Laud. They believed that a compromise might have been reached and that their master was overhasty. But tactful compromise was not one of Charles's characteristics. He resolved to renew the war against the Scots without parliamentary aid.

Strafford agreed that the war against the Scots must be resumed, but he and most of the royal counsellors were justifiably pessimistic about its result. Strafford himself was appointed Commander-in-Chief of the army, but he was laid low with dysentery, pleurisy and stone and had to be carried north in a litter. 'Never', he declared, 'came any man to so mightily lost a business.' This time the Scots did not wait to be invaded, but crossed the Tyne to rout the English cavalry. In humiliation the King was obliged to accept the Treaty of Ripon (21 October 1640) by which he agreed to allow the Scottish army to remain in Northumberland and Durham and to pay its expenses there until final terms were settled. Unjustly Charles blamed Strafford for the failure of his second campaign against the Scots. Now the King had no alternative but to call another Parliament to Westminster. The meeting of this Parliament – to be known as the Long Parliament – on 3 November 1640 led directly to the civil wars in England.

The House of Commons during the 'Short Parliament', which assembled on 13 April 1640 and had sat for less than a month when Charles dissolved it on 4 May. On either side are the thirty-eight boroughs represented in Parliament.

Chapter Three

THE WAR OPENS 1640–1642

No serious evidence has yet been discovered to prove that John Pym or anyone else campaigned to influence the character of the Parliament that met at Westminster in the late autumn of 1640. A historian who has examined the question closely writes: 'no band of revolutionaries were these, the men of England's revolutionary parliament'. It was composed, much in the way that the Short Parliament and other Parliaments had been, chiefly of leading country gentlemen, many of whom were related to one another. To give one or two examples: Denzil Holles, the member for Dorchester, who had been a strong opponent of ship money and was to become (until 1647) a critic of the King's Government, was the second cousin of Gervase Holles, a member for Grimsby, who was to show himself later to be a Royalist. Sir Edward Dering, a member for the county of Kent, who was also to become a Royalist, was related to Sir Henry Vane the Younger, in later years to emerge as a prominent republican. Bulstrode Whitelocke, the member for Great Marlow, by profession a lawyer, who was to figure importantly in the future republican administration, was related to Sir Edward Hyde, a member for Cornwall who was to be one of the most loyal adherents of Charles I and his son. But at the time nearly all of these men were well-to-do subjects and at first were equally critical of the King's policies. It has been estimated that not more than fifty members of the House of Commons were courtiers or royal officials, but even if they were, that did not necessarily mean that they approved the King's domestic, foreign or religious programme. For instance, Sir Edmund Verney, who held the office of Knight Marshal of the Household and was to die fighting for the King, 'voted steadily in opposition to Charles's wishes'. At least nine-tenths of the Commons were critical of the King's 'evil counsellors'.

The general atmosphere of the time was one of restlessness and uncertainty brought about not only by a trade depression, unemployment and plague but also by the presence of the Covenanter army on English soil. In London the senior alderman, who was

Londoners fleeing from the plague.

Two of the London tradesmen active as lay-preachers.

known to be loyal to the Government, was rejected as Lord Mayor in favour of a compromise candidate; the Recorder for London, whom the King wanted to be chosen Speaker of the House of Commons, was not elected a member of parliament for the City and all four City members were Puritans known to be highly critical of the Government. Yet the City officials as a whole were by no means disloyal; it was the London shopkeepers and apprentices and, as the King was to declare later, 'the meaner sorts of people' who first showed themselves to be disorderly and dissatisfied with the King's Government.

The King himself made the opening speech to Parliament in which he insisted that the Scots were rebels and that Parliament must provide money to pay for his army so as to get rid of the Scots. Charles I was aware that most of his Ministers were broken reeds. The Lord Keeper, Finch, in addressing the new Parliament, claimed that the Scottish war had been approved by the whole of the Privy Council and thus implicitly laid the blame for its initiation on the King himself. Charles had understandably called upon the Earl of Strafford, the only really strong man in his Privy Council, to come up to London to lend him his support. Strafford had no illusions about his task. When he left his home to go to Westminster on 6 November he declared that he was going to London 'with more danger beset, I believe, than ever man went out of Yorkshire'. He disapproved of Finch's speech and regarded it as his duty to defend the King's policy towards the Scots and face any charges that Pym and the Commons chose to bring against him. On the very day after Strafford took his seat in the House of Lords Pym announced his intention of impeaching him for treason. Other advisers of the King, including Laud, were also attacked as 'evil counsellors', but Strafford's case was deliberately selected as a trial of strength between the majority of the Commons and Charles I.

Though Strafford was thus the main objective of the movement against the Government and the strategy adopted by both sides was to make him the scapegoat, it must be understood that the accumulation of grievances since Charles I came to the throne and during the

48

John Pym (1584–1643), the leader of parliamentary opposition to Charles I and his Government, painted by Samuel Cooper (*see also* p. 61).

long intermission between Parliaments was what created an atmosphere of near unanimity in Parliament. In his speech Pym wove these grievances together and complained of attacks on parliamentary privileges, innovations in religion, and the invasions of the liberties of subjects by the enforcement of illegal taxation. It was the very breadth of these grievances that enabled Pym in a House of Commons which contained many future Royalists to keep the House united. Hyde, for example, as a practising lawyer, condemned the prerogative courts; Lord Falkland blamed the Bench of Judges for permitting the King to collect ship money; Sir Edward Dering was angry over clerical abuses; Sir John Culpeper stigmatized 'monopolists' as 'the frogs of Egypt' who 'sup in our cup, dip in our dish and sit by our fire'. But Pym was the man who held everything together. He realized that once the King's Ministers had been overthrown – and the mere threat of impeachment caused two or three of them to flee the country – the supremacy of Parliament would be established and the roots of sovereignty undermined.

Pym therefore refused to be diverted by questions of religious organization about which the Commons were not unanimous and managed to get a proposal to abolish the bishops, sponsored by Henry Vane the Younger and Oliver Cromwell, one of the members for Cambridge, put on one side. On the other hand, he approved of an attempt to legalize the regular meeting of Parliament; and a Bill requiring that Parliament should meet at least once every three years was read in the Commons for the third time in January 1641. It was during this same month that the detailed accusations against Strafford were presented by Pym and his colleagues before the House of Lords. Strafford's trial opened on 22 March, but he defended himself with such vigour and persuasiveness that it soon became doubtful whether the Lords would convict their fellow peer. Most of the charges against him could hardly be described as treasonable, while the evidence that he had given unconstitutional advice to the King was tenuous. By the middle of April Pym and his friends decided to proceed against Strafford not by impeachment but by promoting a Bill of Attainder condemning him to death as a traitor. The advantage of this procedure was that no proof of guilt was necessary; it was sufficient merely to assert that Strafford had severed the ancient harmony between the King and Parliament. The disadvantage of this method was that assent to the Bill would be required not only from the House of Commons (which passed it by a substantial majority) but also from the House of Lords and the King. But they could be intimidated. It was the success of this intimidation that opened the direct road to civil war.

During the last week of April and the beginning of May the King and John Pym manœuvred against each other. Charles assured Strafford that though he would have to dismiss him from the royal service he should not 'suffer in life, honour or fortune'. He then attempted to conciliate Pym and his friends by offering them ministerial positions. When that failed, he summoned the two Houses of Parliament to meet him. In a speech, which even his friends regarded as ill-judged, he insisted that his tender conscience would not allow him to agree to the attainder of Strafford; he appealed particularly to the House of Lords to rescue him from his embarrassment. But his speech made no impact and when next day Charles sent an officer with a hundred men to seize the Tower of London in which Strafford was lodged as a prisoner, the Lieutenant of the Tower, Sir William Balfour, defied his orders. Then the King and Queen thought of moving out of London to take refuge with the remnants of the royal army in the north of England. But as usual Charles was irresolute.

On the other side, City mobs agitated for Strafford's execution. A petition with thousands of signatures demanded the death of a traitor. The names of the minority in the Commons who had voted against the Bill of Attainder were posted up in the City and described as 'betrayers of their country'. Shops were shut; wild rumours circulated; an armed multitude accompanied the members of parliament when they went to ask the King to sign the Bill of Attainder.

Why did the House of Lords pass the Bill? Some members who might have voted against it were too frightened to appear, while others believed that if Strafford escaped, he would raise an army against Parliament. The King too began to fear for the safety of his Queen. He thought that armed mobs might invade his palaces of Whitehall and St James's – as the French mob was to surge into the palaces of Louis XVI a hundred and fifty years later. Strafford himself wrote to the King begging him to sign the Bill of Attainder so that harmony might be restored between him and his subjects. Judges assured Charles that Strafford had indeed been guilty of treason, while a bishop was found to draw a distinction between the King's private and public conscience. On 10 May Charles gave his assent to the Bill; and he signed another Bill for the perpetuation of the existing Parliament with the same pen and ink as he signed away the life of his Minister. Strafford was not even allowed to see his friend, Archbishop Laud, who was also imprisoned in the Tower, before being shepherded to the scaffold on 12 May. Laud himself wrote apropos the death of Strafford that the King 'knew not how to be or be made great'.

Sir William Balfour (d. 1660). As Lieutenant of the Tower of London, he prevented Charles's attempt to free the imprisoned Strafford by force.

Two important questions arise out of the events in the spring of 1641 which were a dress rehearsal for the civil war. The first is of whom did the armed mobs consist that intimidated the King and Strafford's fellow peers into passing the Bill of Attainder? It seems that those who lined the approaches to Westminster Hall on the afternoon of 8 May were mainly respectable merchants, shop-keepers, members of the City of London militia, and apprentices. On the other hand, the crowds who gathered in Palace Yard and outside Whitehall Palace during the readings of the Bill were of a rougher character and included 'ordinary mechanic folk' from Southwark. Plainly when one talks of an armed multitude (unless one is thinking in terms of men simply armed with sticks and clubs) it is pretty certain that those who possessed swords or muskets were better-off citizens. It is likely that the demonstrations were actually organized by members of parliament for the City like Isaac Penington, who were not only fiercely puritanical but were practising merchants influential with the shopkeepers and apprentices in the City companies. It was therefore an alliance between discontented members of the Commons and organized mobs which brought the King to his knees.

The second question is what did Pym and his friends hope to gain by compelling the King to abandon Strafford? Modern historians have concluded that on the whole Pym was loyal to the monarchy, true to the existing constitution, which he believed had been violated by the King's advisers, and in general was leader of a moderate party which aimed to uphold the prevailing structure of society. These moderates, it has been contended, were conservatives who only wanted to restore order in the Church and State as it had been in the good old days. Pym, wrote Gardiner, was 'purely conservative' and constituted himself 'the guardian of the old religion and the old law'. But the fact remained that his clear object was (however he may have phrased it) to strengthen the position of

Parliament at the expense of the monarchy. Before he died he was not only to ensure the constitutional irremovability of the House of Commons in which he reigned supreme but also to require that the King surrender his power over the army and allow his Ministers to be chosen for him by Parliament. Pym was not an emotional man; he was patient and deliberate in his behaviour and convinced that the House of Commons was or should be the soul of the body politic. As Veronica Wedgwood has justly observed, what men like Pym and his friends, John Hampden and Oliver St John, were aiming at was not merely the removal of Strafford and the King's other 'evil counsellors' but 'the transference of effective power from the King's hands into that of the High Court of Parliament'. They might refer back to the murky days of King John and his son for precedents, but in reality their aims were revolutionary.

The impeachment of the Earl of Strafford in 1641, by the Commons before the House of Lords. Strafford is seen from the back standing in the dock, in the centre near the bottom of the picture.

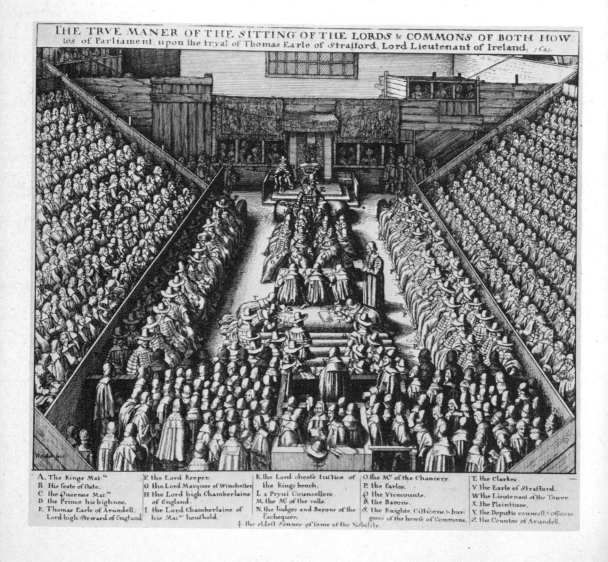

THE TRVE MANER OF THE SITTING OF THE LORDS & COMMONS OF BOTH HOW-
les of Parliament, upon the tryal of Thomas Earle of Stratford, Lord Lieutenant of Ireland, 1641.

A. The Kings Maⁱᵉ
B. His seate of state.
C. the Queenes Maⁱᵉ
D. the Prince his highnes.
E. Thomas Earle of Arundell, Lord high Steward of England

F. the Lord Keeper.
G. the Lord Marquess of Winchester
H. the Lord high Chamberlaine of England
I. the Lord Chamberlaine of his Maⁱᵉˢ houshold.

K. the Lord cheefe Justice of the Kings bench,
L. 2 Pryui Councellors,
M. the Mʳ of the rolls.
N. the Iudges and Barons of the Exchequer.
† the oldest Sonnes of some of the Nobility.

O. the Mʳˢ of the Chancery.
P. the Earles.
Q. the Vicecounts,
R. the Barons.
S. the Knights, Cittizens, & bur-geses of the howse of Commons,

T. the Clarkes.
V. the Earle of Stratford.
W. the Lieutenant of the Tower.
X. the Plaintiues,
Y. the Deputts councell & officers.
Z. the Countes of Arundell.

A. Doctor Vsher. Lord Prim
te of Ireland.
B the Sherifes of London
C the Earle of Strafford
D. his kindred and friends

'The summer of 1641', it has been said, 'was a time of play-acting and changes of mood.' Pym purposed to follow up his triumph against Strafford by introducing constitutional reforms and reducing the royal prerogatives. In order to do so he had to prevent quarrels arising between the two Houses of Parliament as well as stopping the Commons from sinking into a morass of private Bills and religious disputes. For his part the King hoped that if he continued to grant concessions a reaction would set in to his advantage. He might even be able to retain his rights by force, for he still had the army formed by Strafford in Ireland and his own army in the north of England; he might also be able to come to terms with the Covenanter army. Convinced that he ruled by divine right, he hoped that in God's own good time his former position of authority would be restored, if necessary by duress.

So during June and July Charles gracefully made concessions. He had already agreed that Parliament could not be dissolved without its own consent and that in future Parliaments would be called regularly, specific provisions being included in a Triennial Act which allowed Parliament to be summoned without the King's orders. Tonnage and poundage were in future to be voted only for very short periods and the yield from these duties was to be kept under the close supervision of the Commons. Ship money was declared illegal. Money voted for the payment of the Scottish army was not to be handed over to the Treasury but paid directly to the

Strafford was beheaded on Tower Hill on 12 May 1641. Hollar recorded the scene (*top*), and a commemorative medal was designed, bearing a portrait based on Van Dyck's painting (*see* p. 45).

53

City of London which had raised a loan for the purpose of its upkeep. Conciliar jurisdiction was thenceforward abolished in all its forms: this meant that both the Court of Star Chamber, instituted by the Tudors to deal with over-powerful subjects, and the High Commission, which was created to sustain the authority of the Church, now ceased to exist. The King repudiated friends of his who both in England and Scotland concocted or tried to concoct military plans on his behalf. Furthermore he promoted the third Earl of Essex, an enthusiastic Puritan who had been active in hounding Strafford to his death, to be his Lord Chamberlain.

How far the King really followed any consistent policy at this stage has been disputed. It has been asserted that he oscillated between concessions and intrigues. What does seem pretty clear is that he regarded everything he yielded under pressure from the House of Commons as indulgences conferred while he was playing for time to win back his authority. In assenting to the Triennial Bill, for example, he said that 'never a Bill passed here was of more favour to subjects than this is', but added, 'you have taken the government all in pieces and I may say off its hinges . . .'. This was the kind of language to arouse suspicions and increase the influence of those who still felt that Charles was not to be trusted. But on the other hand at the same time the campaign of religious extremists – as exemplified by a 'root-and-branch' Bill put forward to abolish bishops and deans as well as an attempt that was made to exclude bishops from the House of Lords – not only alienated peers, as trenching upon their historic rights, but antagonized moderate members of the Church such as Lord Falkland and Edward Hyde in the Commons. These men cannot yet be described as Royalists, but they were coming to believe that constitutional reform had gone far enough; they genuinely wanted to reconcile monarchy and Parliament; and they themselves were willing to accept ministerial offices, thus becoming the agents of such a reconciliation.

But Pym clung to a more revolutionary point of view. When the King announced that he had decided to visit Scotland early in August after a settlement had at last been reached with the Covenanters, the Commons not only set up a committee to supervise the defence of the realm, but selected a number of Commissioners to follow Charles to Scotland, that is to say in effect to spy upon his movements. When Parliament adjourned for six weeks the two Houses appointed a committee, over which Pym himself presided, to manage business during the recess, to arrange for the demobilization of the King's army, and to keep in touch with the Commissioners sent to Scotland. Moreover Pym and his friends were now determined to ensure the expansion of parliamentary authority not merely while the Houses were in recess but for all time by claiming the right to nominate or approve all the King's Ministers and military officers.

Parliament reassembled on 20 October 1641 while the King was still in Scotland graciously bestowing concessions on all and sundry.

Opposite: Robert Devereux, third Earl of Essex (1591–1646). Charles attempted to conciliate the Puritans by making him Lord Chamberlain, but when war came his title and experience in the Thirty Years' War made him a natural choice for leader of the Parliamentarian forces. A proud and melancholy man, he set off for his first engagement 'carrying with him his coffin and winding-sheet, together with the escutcheon which would be needed at his funeral'.

A MAP OF Y KINGDOME OF IRELAND.
With perticuler notes distinguishing the Townes revolted taken or burnt since the late Rebellion

The panic aroused by the Irish rebellion of 1641–42 was reflected in a number of prints and pamphlets issued in London by Puritan sympathizers. Seen here are a map of Ireland (*right*) purporting to show 'the Townes revolted, taken or burnt' during the rebellion, and (*opposite*) the title-page of a pamphlet relating 'plots which were contrived and hatched in Ireland' and the attempt on the life of the informer, 'Owen Ockanellee'.

Within a fortnight members learned the news that a rebellion had broken out in Ulster where the native Irish seized arms, plundered the English settlers and threatened to advance on Dublin, partly because they feared that it was the intention of the Lords Justice, who had ruled there since the death of Strafford, to extirpate the Roman Catholic religion and partly because they were provoked by hatred of intruders who kept them ground down by poverty. At Westminster Pym grasped the opportunity provided by grossly exaggerated stories of Irish massacres, which he blamed on the incompetence of the King's Ministers and the Catholic predilections of the Court, to put forward his own panacea. On 5 November he moved that unless Charles agreed to dismiss those of his counsellors

An Exact and true Relation
of the late Plots which were con-
trived and hatched in *Ireland*.

1. A Coppy of a Letter sent from the Lord chiefe Iustices and Privy Councell in *Ireland*, to our parliament here in *England*.

2. Their last Proclamation which they published concerning those Traytors.

3. The whole Discourse of the Plot revealed by *Owen Ockanellee* who is now in *Englond*.

4. The dangerous and extraordinary deliverance of the party who narrowly escaped with his life.

5. The reward the Parliament hath confirmed upon him.

6. The true Relation of the whole Treason related by the Lord Keeper, to the Honourable House of Commons the first of *November*. 1641.

London Printed for *Francis Coules*, 1641.

who were at fault and replace them with advisers approved by Parliament the Commons should offer no assistance in suppressing the Irish rebellion. On the following day Oliver Cromwell moved that the Earl of Essex should be empowered by 'an ordinance of Parliament' and not by the instructions of the monarch to take command of the English militia in order to defend the kingdom and that he should continue to do so until Parliament decided otherwise. Thus the House of Commons endorsed two far-reaching proposi-tions: first, that the King should 'employ only such counsellors and ministers as should be approved by Parliament'; secondly, that Parliament and not the King should supervise the defence of the realm.

Hampton Court, the Tudor
palace outside London to
which Charles withdrew
with his family in January
1641, and where he was held
prisoner in 1647. Later,
Cromwell used the palace as
his country residence when
he was Lord Protector.

Pym's motion that the King should only employ Ministers
approved by Parliament was carried in the Commons by 151 votes
to 110. Immediately afterwards Pym introduced a 'Grand Remonstrance' in which all the grievances against the Government during
Charles I's reign were listed as a manifesto to the nation; not only
were all the past political failures set out – for example, wars mis-
managed by Buckingham – but the assertion was made that the
'fundamental laws' of the kingdom had been undermined and a
Popish conspiracy fomented to divide the King from his people.
In the debates on the Remonstrance the main opposition was displayed over the religious clauses. Edward Hyde did not deny that
the catalogue of grievances was true, but he considered that to
rehash their history was pointless and tactless. Some members
thought that it was ridiculous to say that the Book of Common
Prayer contained superstititions; and others denied that bishops
were idolaters. Eventually the Remonstrance was approved at
midnight on 22 November by a mere 159 votes to 148. Oliver
Cromwell declared that had it not been passed he and other members
would have left England forever.

The House of Commons consisted of over five hundred members:
out of that number only three hundred steadily attended the debates.
The votes in November showed that the three hundred were almost
equally divided over questions of politics and religion. But the
leaders of the majority maintained that it was iniquitous to suggest
that the House was divided at all; was it not a Great Council of the
Realm comparable to the seamless robe of Christ? Two men were
actually sent to the Tower for admitting that there were 'two sides'
in the House. Yet it was absurd to pretend otherwise. Charles I,
when he returned to London from Scotland three days after the
Grand Remonstrance was carried, recognized the obvious situation

Colonell Lunsford assaulting the Londoners at Westminster Hall, with a great rout of ruffinly Cavaleiros

Demonstrations in London against royal authority and Popery were at first quickly put down. *Below:* the Earl of Dorset (1591–1652), a veteran of the Thirty Years War, who crushed the demonstration at Westminster in November 1641. *Left:* Colonel Lunsford 'with a great rout of ruffianly Cavaliers' dispersing Londoners at Westminster Hall.

and for that reason was at last emboldened to stand firmly for his rights. He was welcomed by the official authorities in the City of London, which now had a Lord Mayor friendly to him. As if to emphasize his aloofness he retired to the Tudor palace of Hampton Court outside London where he was visited by a deputation from the majority in the Commons who invited him to accept the Remonstrance and let Parliament henceforward appoint his Ministers. The King retorted by depriving the Earl of Essex of his post of Commander-in-Chief, relieving the London militia of the duty of guarding Parliament, replacing it with loyal halberdiers under the Earl of Dorset, and on 21 December removing Balfour from the lieutenancy of the Tower. He also issued a declaration on religion, upholding the Book of Common Prayer, and named new bishops to fill empty sees.

This challenge to Parliament or resumption of the royal authority was met by a fresh demonstration by Penington and his friends in the City. After an armed demonstration gathered at Westminster on 29 November crying out 'No Popery!' it was firmly dealt with by the Earl of Dorset. When a fortnight later a petition was brought from the City demanding the exclusion of the bishops from the House of Lords and asking that the control over the militia be transferred from the King to Parliament, only a hundred petitioners were allowed into the House of Commons to put their case. On 10 December the Commons again revealed their divisions, for the motion to take away the control of the militia from the King was carried by 158 votes to 125. The King saw his chance. On 14 December he came to the House of Lords to say that he would only pass the Militia Bill if his rights were respected. On 23 December he in effect rejected the Grand Remonstrance passed in the Commons (which, much to his annoyance, had been printed); he stood by the

> *six*   20
>
> 1 You ar to accuse thofe ~~figure~~ ioynt lie & feuerallie
> 2 you ar to referue the power of making addicionall
> 3 When the Comitie for examination is a naming (wch you
>   must prefs to be clofe & under tey of fecresie) if eather
>   Effex, Warwick, Holland, Say, ~~[struck out]~~ Wharton, or
>   Brooke be named, you must defyre that they may be spared
>   because you ar to examine them as witneffes for me

King Charles's instructions
to his Attorney-General for
the impeachment of leading
members of parliament,
3 January 1642.

Church of England and the traditional rights of the English monarchy. Thus were the lines of battle clearly drawn.

The crux came during the twelve days of Christmas. Agitations swept the City. The stairs from the River Thames to Palace Yard were crowded with citizens who aimed to prevent bishops from landing there to take their seats in the House of Lords. Apprentices flooded Whitehall. The King, though giving way to protests over the lieutenancy of the Tower, saw that it stayed in the hands of a man he could trust. Finally Charles made up his mind to impeach Pym and four other members of the Commons together with one member of the House of Lords – Lord Mandeville (the future Earl of Manchester and Parliamentarian commander) – for treason. The majority of the peers, though sympathetic to the King, doubted his claim to impeach: indeed it was thought to be a violation of their own rights. Therefore his request that they should order the arrest of members of parliament was refused. On 4 January 1642 Charles decided to act on his own responsibility. But by the time he entered the House of Commons that evening, had taken off his hat, and occupied the Speaker's chair, the five accused members had departed by barge down the river. Their friends hid them safely in the heart of the City. Six days later, realizing that he had been outmanoeuvred, the King removed his family from Whitehall to Hampton Court. He was not to return to London until he himself was put on trial seven years later.

When did the civil war become inevitable? Notions of inevitability are best left to predestinarians. What is sure is that preparations for war began as soon as the King left London. In January Charles ordered the Earl of Newcastle to assume the governorship of the port of Hull; he also tried to obtain control of Portsmouth and of the Tower of London and aimed to lay hold of the Surrey magazine

Opposite: a pamphlet
printing Pym's victorious
speech, after the failure of
the King's attempted
impeachment. (It is dated
1641 because the calendar
year ran from March to
March.)

Maſter PYM

HISSPEECH

In *Parliament*, on *Wedneſday*, the
fifth of *January*, 1641,

Concerning the Vote of the House of *Commons*,
for his diſcharge upon the Accuſation of High
Treaſon, exhibited againſt himſelfe, and the
Lord *Kimbolton*, Mr. *Iohn Hampden*, Sr.
Arthur Hiſlerig, Mr. *Strowd*,
M. Hollis, by his Maieſty.

The true Effigies of Mr. *Iohn Pym*, Eſquire

London Printed for I.W. 1641.

William Cavendish, Earl, Marquis and later first Duke of Newcastle (1593–1676), one of the richest men in England. His appointment as Governor of Hull was one of Charles's first acts in preparation for civil war. Newcastle commanded the Royalist forces in the north until 1644, withdrawing abroad after the defeat at Marston Moor.

at Kingston upon Thames. On 23 February the Queen secretly left England, nominally to attend the wedding of her daughter Mary in Holland, but in reality to pawn Crown jewels with which to buy arms. But John Pym, now known as 'King Pym', was extremely vigilant and frustrated all the royal plans except that he could not prevent the Queen's departure. On 12 February the two Houses of Parliament agreed upon a list of persons whom they recommended as Lords-Lieutenant of the counties. The principal duty of these officers was to concern themselves with the recruiting of the militia and questions of local defence. To make assurance doubly sure three days later an Ordinance was introduced into the House of Commons whereby the control of the militia was to be transferred from the King to Parliament.

Though each side was thus already preparing for war, negotiations between Parliament and the King continued until March. On 13 February Charles actually gave his assent to a Bill to exclude the bishops from the House of Lords: he also promised to enforce the penal laws against Roman Catholics and he agreed to a Bill impressing soldiers to go to Ireland. The Queen had been largely responsible for inducing her husband to make these concessions, hoping that they would buy time while she was away. But she had also insisted that the King should not on any account give up his control over the militia. He made that clear in an interview with the Earl of Pembroke at the end of February. Asked to agree to abandoning his control

temporarily, Charles answered 'By God, not for an hour.' The preamble to the Militia Ordinance drawn up in the Commons affirmed that 'the High Court of Parliament is not only the Court of Judicature, enabled by the laws to adjudge and determine the rights and liberties of the Kingdom . . . but is likewise a Council to provide for the necessity, to prevent the imminent dangers, and preserve the public peace and safety of the kingdom'. Thus by March the two constitutional positions had been plainly defined. The King refused to give up his prerogatives; Parliament sought ultimate sovereignty. By 22 March the Militia Ordinance had been passed by both Houses, the claim being asserted that it was valid without the royal assent. The question of the power of the sword was the breaking point in a contest of wills which stretched over two years.

By May the King had set up his headquarters in York where he summoned peers, judges and members of parliament to join him, and early in June Commissioners from Westminster carried their peace terms known as 'the nineteen propositions' to him there. These propositions demanded the right of Parliament to appoint the King's Ministers, officials and judges; they required the King to agree to Parliament reforming the Church; and they asked for complete control of the castles and fortresses throughout the kingdom together with the dismissal of his personal guards. To this ultimatum, which in effect claimed full sovereignty for Parliament and left the King as a figurehead, Charles answered by adopting the

A Dutch medal struck to commemorate Queen Henrietta Maria's voyage to Holland in February 1642 shows a ship on rough seas steering close to a rock, with the legend *mediis immota procellis* (unmoved amidst storms).

63

attitude that there should be a partnership between him and Parliament. For in reply he adumbrated a doctrine known as 'mixed monarchy' which would have been extremely distasteful to his father. He and his propagandists insisted that he did not seek absolute power or 'an arbitrary way of government' but merely a reversion to the ancient constitution under which the country was governed by the King in Parliament.

The nineteen propositions and the King's answer to them comprised a battle of words that led nowhere. In July Parliament appointed the Earl of Warwick to take command of the navy and the Earl of Essex to be general of a Parliamentarian army. The best that the King could do was to seize the port of Newcastle upon Tyne, to borrow money from some wealthy peers, and to issue commissions of array in the hope of recruiting soldiers in defiance of the arrangements being carried out on behalf of Parliament. As early as March the recruiting efforts undertaken by rival Lords-Lieutenant in Lancashire resulted in the spilling of blood at the small town of Manchester. Parliament had already set up a Committee of Safety, composed of members of both Houses, to defend the kingdom against the King. Charles retorted by calling upon his loyal subjects to restore his authority. On 22 August the royal standard was formally raised in Nottingham and the civil war began.

Charles I in armour, dictating to his Secretary-at-War Sir Edward Walker. The setting is thought to be the country around Nottingham, where the King raised his standard and the civil war began.

Chapter Four

FIRST CAMPAIGNS 1642–1643

'On the whole,' wrote Gardiner nearly ninety years ago, 'the nobility and gentry took the side of the King, whilst townsmen and yeomanry took the side of Parliament.' Historians have been embroidering on that text ever since. We have seen that though the generalization can be sustained to a limited extent by literary evidence, close examination of county histories proves conclusively that the civil war was not a class war. The Earls of Bedford, Essex, Manchester, Northumberland, Pembroke, Peterborough and Warwick all served Parliament and all except Pembroke held high military commands. Though a majority of peers understandably sympathized with the King, the gentry were divided down the middle. To give a few examples: among the gentry of Cornwall Lord Robartes, Sir Richard Buller and Edmund Prideaux were for Parliament, Sir Francis Godolphin, Sir John Arundel and Sir Charles Trevanion were for the King. In Kent Sir Anthony Weldon, Sir Michael Livsey and Sir John Sedley were for Parliament, while Sir John Culpeper, Sir Roger Twysden and Sir Edward Dering were for the King. In Somerset Alexander Popham, John Pyne and William Strode – all well-to-do landlords – were keen Parliamentarians, while Sir Ralph Hopton, Sir John Poulett and Sir John Stawell were active Royalists.

Even families were not united in their loyalties. Writing for the benefit of his descendants, Sir John Oglander, a Royalist in the Isle of Wight, observed: 'Thou wouldst think it strange if I should tell thee there was a time in England when brothers killed brothers, cousins, cousins and friends their friends.' That was literally true. Charles Fleetwood, a leading Parliamentarian officer, had a brother, Walter, who was a faithful Royalist; Sir Richard Feilding, who held Reading for the King in 1643, had an elder brother, Basil, who was fighting for Parliament. Sir Henry Vane, who was to become a dyed-in-the-wool republican, had a younger brother, Walter, who was a Royalist. Ralph Verney was told by his brother, Sir Edmund, the Knight Marshal of the King's Household, that his being against the King was

Friends divided by the war: the Royalist Sir Ralph Hopton (1598–1652), *left*, and Sir William Waller (1597–1668), one of the most brilliant Parliamentarian commanders.

Opposite: London in the early years of the war. *Above:* the 'idolatrous Cross' of Cheapside is pulled down in 1643, to the sound of trumpets and 'a great shout of people with joy'. *Below:* the city and suburbs fortified by Parliament in 1642–43. Strongpoints included Shoreditch (4, 5), the New River pond in Islington (9), Hyde Park Corner (16) and Vauxhall (20).

'most unhandsomely done' and that he regretted he must be his brother's enemy. Denzil Holles, a defiant and wealthy critic of the monarchical Government's policies in Church and State, had three cousins who were Royalists. In Yorkshire Sir Thomas Mauleverer raised three regiments for Parliament and was to sign the King's death warrant, but his son Richard fought for Charles and was imprisoned for his loyalty. Two commanders who fought on opposite sides during the war, Sir Ralph Hopton of Somerset and Sir William Waller, a Devonian, had been close friends and confessed that they were fighting 'a war without an enemy'.

The rich were not necessarily on the King's side. Although he was supported by two fabulously wealthy peers, the Earl of Newcastle and the Marquis of Worcester, it was on the whole in the poorer parts that most Royalists were to be found. It is dangerous to be too emphatic about the political complexion of the counties. While it is true that on the whole the west of England, the west Midlands, the East Riding of Yorkshire and the far northern counties were Royalist, while the home counties, eastern and south-eastern England were Parliamentarian, that was not always because of public opinion but because of the complications of regional affairs and family rivalries; moreover changes of attitude might be brought about by military pressures from without or changes in the fortunes of war within. For instance, Somerset was said to be Parliamentarian in 1642 and Royalist in 1643, largely because of an invasion from Cornwall. On the other hand, Kent was Royalist in 1642 and became Parliamentarian by 1643 in consequence of a military expedition dispatched there from Westminster. London itself – at any rate official London – was still Royalist during the first half of 1642, but by August 1643, owing to a *coup d'état* in the City, engineered from the House of Commons which impeached the Royalist Lord Mayor, it became Parliamentarian in sympathy and remained so for ten years or more.

Finally, it should be noted that the ports and towns in the kingdom and the merchant princes of the time were not necessarily Royalist. When the war began Portsmouth, Newcastle and Chester, three busy ports, were under Royalist control. London, as has been noticed, was divided in its allegiance, while Bristol changed sides as a result of military action in 1643. Such merchants as had seats in the House of Commons, usually as representatives of boroughs, were equally divided in their loyalties; though some London financiers backed Parliament in 1642 because they resented the levying of Customs duties by the Crown without Parliament's consent, they were soon to discover that direct and indirect taxes introduced by 'King Pym' were heavier than anything that King Charles had imposed; by the end of the Interregnum the City was pretty solidly Royalist.

Since the beginning of 1642 both sides had been recruiting and collecting supplies. On paper the army serving under the Earl of Essex was formidable. Essex himself owed his position as much to

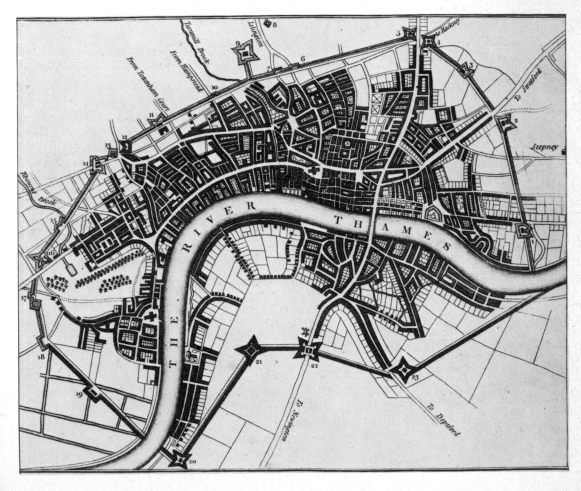

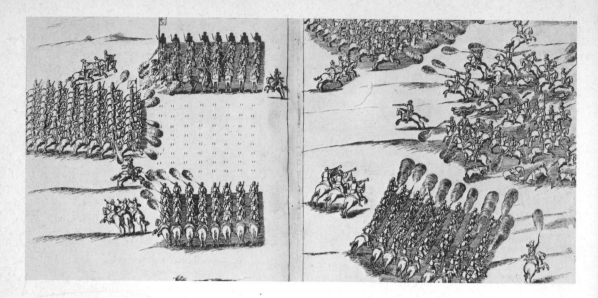

Illustrations from *Militarie Instructions for the Cavallrie* by John Cruso (1632), showing forms of attack and defence, and contemporary cavalry armour.

Opposite: Prince Rupert (1619–82), Charles I's nephew whom he appointed General of the Horse at the outbreak of the war. Dobson's painting shows him when he was about twenty-five.

his title as to the experience he acquired through having served in the Netherlands. He was a proud, indolent and melancholy man. As to his skill as a general, it has justly been pointed out by a modern military critic that he managed to fight three battles in positions where his enemy had cut him off from his base. (Cromwell also was to do so at the battle of Dunbar, but there his forces could be supplied by sea.) Charles I was his own Commander-in-Chief; his abilities have been underestimated. At least he had the right ideas, but he was a poor judge of men. He relied unduly upon cautious and aged professionals like Lord Forth. He never entirely trusted his brilliant young nephew, Prince Rupert of the Palatinate, who though only twenty-three was already an experienced soldier and came over to England at the start of the civil war to aid his uncle. Charles was to give him misleading orders and unjustified reprimands. The Earl of Essex had at his disposal six cavalry regiments, nineteen regiments of infantry and five troops of dragoons or mounted infantry, altogether some 15,000 men. On both sides an infantry regiment numbered or was supposed to number about 1,200 men and a cavalry regiment 300 or 400 men. Infantry regiments had both musketeers and pikemen armed with clumsy weapons. The cavalry were heavy rather than light, wore armour and were relatively well paid; their action determined the result of most battles. As to the artillery, the heavy field-guns fired only about twelve times an hour and could hardly have played a significant part in the war except at sieges.

At the outset of the war the King had eight cavalry regiments, fifteen regiments of infantry and one of dragoons, a total of some 13,500 men, but the regiments were rarely up to strength. By the time that the battle of Naseby was fought in 1645 twenty of the so-called northern regiments serving the King had an average of only

a hundred men each. To begin with the Royalist cavalry were better equipped and better trained than those of the Parliamentarians. Neither side had much initial difficulty over recruiting, for 1642 was a year of depression and men enlisted for money as well as excitement. But discipline was poor on both sides. For though such professional officers as there were (who had mostly learned their trade abroad, some of them simply as volunteers in search of adventure) recognized the necessity of training in skirmishing as well as in drill, the first campaign began suddenly at an unusual time of the year when the harvests were still being brought in. Thus few opportunities occurred for more than rudimentary preparations; only the eight regiments of the London militia had undergone thorough training. Moreover when the war broke out a number of officers were still awaiting their commissions before they could start recruiting and exercising their men.

One other important factor was that the whole of the navy on which Charles had lavished the proceeds of the unpopular ship money declared itself for Parliament. In January 1642 2,000 mariners had marched into London to offer their services to Parliament. They were partly motivated by fear of Popery. In a protestation they referred to the 'rocks of Rome' and the 'quicksands of Spain', but no doubt the King's failure to pay his seamen punctually and regularly also alienated them from him. However, it is doubtful whether command of the sea was a decisive influence on the course of the first civil war, though it certainly was in the second and third civil wars. It was significant only in a negative sense: for had the royal navy been true to the King, he might have blockaded London and thus forced it into submission. As it was, Parliament's hold on the capital was crucial to its ultimate success in the civil wars.

Before the first battle of the war was fought both sides manoeuvred for position. On 13 September Charles left Nottingham and a week later arrived at Shrewsbury. Thence he darted north to secure Chester where troops from Ireland might be landed. Meanwhile the Earl of Essex had left London on 9 September, 'carrying with him his coffin and winding-sheet, together with the escutcheon which would be needed at his funeral', to reach Northampton four days later with a sizeable army. Two days afterwards he moved west and occupied Worcester on 21 September. Essex had originally hoped to confront the King at Nottingham and compel him to return to Westminster, but ill-founded rumours diverted him to Worcester. What in fact had happened was that a small Royalist force under Sir John Byron had arrived there from Oxford and Prince Rupert also with a small body of horse had ridden to meet him. A parliamentary detachment under Nathaniel Fiennes, sent in advance by the Earl of Essex, was surprised and beaten up. Fiennes was no soldier and his troopers were raw. The skirmish raised Royalist morale. But King Charles believed that the Parliamentarian army outnumbered his own and each army felt its way cautiously.

The Royalists then sought to move towards London, avoiding towns like Coventry, known to be garrisoned by Parliamentarians, while Essex advanced on a line parallel to that of the King southwards from Worcester and west of the line of the Royalist march. As Edward Hyde, who accompanied the King, wrote afterwards, though 'the two armies were but twenty miles asunder when they set forth and both marched the same way they gave not the least disquiet in ten days march to each other; and in truth, as it appeared afterwards, neither side knew where the other was.' On Saturday 22 October the King was contemplating a halt at Edgecote (forty miles west of Bedford) while a detachment occupied Banbury. But that night Charles received a message from Prince Rupert that the Earl of Essex was on his track and indeed that the enemy army was only seven miles to his west. Next morning the King ordered his own army to occupy Edgehill which dominated the Warwickshire plain.

Sir John Byron (c. 1600–1652), who fought at Powick Bridge and commanded a regiment of horse at Edgehill. Detail of a portrait by Dobson.

Rupert, whom the King had appointed as his General of Horse, immediately showed himself to be the most energetic of the royal officers and military advisers. He had already begun training the cavalry; he had raided Leicester to collect money for the King, an action which was at once disapproved; he had demonstrated his resource at Powick Bridge, where Fiennes had been surprised; he had acted as leader of a reconnaissance force during the advance south; and it was he who suggested the occupation of Edgehill. But being young, he was tactless. He insisted on receiving his orders directly from the King, thus upsetting the over-all commander or General-in-Chief Lord Lindsey; furthermore Charles ordered Lord Forth, a veteran Scottish soldier, to draw up the army ready for battle, whereupon Lindsey resigned to fight and die as a mere colonel. Undoubtedly the hope was that Essex would launch his forces uphill against the royal army; but it seems that Essex wanted the King to strike first so that he might be saddled with the blame for starting full-scale hostilities. The Royalists, who were extremely confident, were therefore obliged to move under the cover of cannon-fire down from Edgehill into the plain where they were redeployed. The battle began in the afternoon when Essex ordered his guns to open fire.

The two armies were roughly equal in size, though the Royalists were slightly stronger in cavalry. Officers then had neither watches nor adequate maps. Consequently it was extremely difficult to synchronize attacks once the trumpets had sounded the advance. This consideration applied to all the battles of the civil wars and it explains why over-all commanders could plan their tactics only along very general lines; once the fighting began they had to rely on their subordinate officers to act as best they could. At Edgehill Rupert, who commanded the Royalist right wing – on each side both wings consisted of cavalry with the infantry massed in the centre – bore down steadily sword in hand on the Parliamentarians opposite him; they vainly discharged their carbines and received little help from small groups of infantry who after the Swedish fashion were interspersed between their squadrons. The fury of the charge carried the Royalists too far forward under the mistaken impression that their enemy was everywhere in retreat. Many of the Royalist troopers engaged in pillaging the Parliamentarians' baggage train three miles to the rear in the village of Kineton. The Royalist charge on the left was equally successful and again the troopers swept on to Kineton. Rupert managed to halt three of his troops and on the left Lieutenant-Colonel Sir Charles Lucas rallied 200 other cavalrymen. But these were by no means sufficient in number to come to the decisive help of the infantry which was engaged in a stiff struggle with the Parliamentarians in the centre. Some untrained parliamentary soldiers panicked; the musketeers were of little use; but massed 'hedgehogs' of pikemen fought hard and bravely. In the end these infantrymen, materially assisted by the intact cavalry regiment of Sir William Balfour, which had been held in reserve and thus avoided the charge on the left, thrust the Royalist foot soldiers back towards Edgehill and put their guns out of action. Only the belated return of Prince Rupert's cavalry to the field of battle and the active intervention of the King himself prevented the cavalry victory from being transformed into an infantry defeat. Finally, as it grew dark, both sides were too exhausted

Edgehill, Warwickshire, scene of the first major battle of the civil war on 23 October 1642. The King occupied the steep slope in the foreground, the battle itself being fought in the plain below.

A diary entry on the battle of Edgehill by the Dutch engineer Sir Bernard de Gomme, who had been brought to England by Prince Rupert: 'A fight between the Kings and Parliamt. forces att Keynton [Kineton] Marsh by Edgehill. . . . Many sore wounded on both sides. . . .'

Below: a Royalist military reward commemorating the presence at Edgehill of Charles, Prince of Wales.

to continue fighting. The two armies encamped on the field, but next day the Royalists returned to their original positions on Edgehill while the Earl of Essex retired to Warwick, his rearguard still harassed by Rupert's cavalry. Technically and actually, therefore, it was a Royalist victory.

Two lessons were learned from the battle of Edgehill. First, the Parliamentarians realized that the King had, after all, been able to recruit a substantial and capable army. The idea that once Charles had been confronted by an armed force raised and financed by Parliament he would be obliged to return to Westminster and accept the peace terms dictated to him had to be abandoned. Thus the decision was taken to reopen negotiations and at the same time to try to persuade a Scottish army to enter the north of England as allies of Parliament. Such persuasion, however, would take time. Secondly, the King understood what war meant. Casualties had been heavy; he had seen loyal officers like Sir Edmund Verney and the Earl of Lindsey die; so he too would have liked an accommodation.

The massed 'hedgehogs' of pikemen at Edgehill.

```
Front
  C
MMMM
MMMM S4
MMMM
  D 2
MMMM
MMMM
MMMM
MMMM
MMMM
  E.
P P P P
P P P P
P P P P
  D 1
P P P P
P P P P
P P P P
P P P P
  S 1
P P P P
P P P P
P P P P
  D 4
P P P P
P P P P
P P P P
P P P P
  S 2
MMMM
MMMM
MMMM
  D 3
MMMM
MMMM
MMMM
MMMM
S3 MMMM
  L
Reere.
```

CHAP. VII.

Of Marching the Company in Divisions, with the order and places of the Officers and Drums.

OVr *Souldiers* now being somewhat *expert* in their *distances*, we wil next draw them forth into a *deepe March*. Where-fore note, that our *files* must be at *order*, and our *Rankes* at *open order* : the *Muskettiers* of the *right flank*, are to make the *Van*, and to *march* next after the *Captaine*; The *Pikes* are to make the *Battell*, and to *march* after the *Ensigne*, either in one or two *divisions*, according to their number. The *Muskettiers* of the *left flank* (some-times called the *second division of Muskets*) make the *Reere Guard*, which is *led* commonly by the *second Serjeant*. Howbeit if there be but one *division* of *Pikes*; then the *eldest* (or chiefest) *Serjeant leads* the *second division of Muskettiers*. If the *Company* bee but *small*: then it is best to make but two *Divisions*, one of the *Muskettiers*, another of the *Pikes*; For the *placing* of the rest of the *Officers*, you may per-ceive by the *figure* in the Margent : Wherefore note that M. stands for *Muskets*, P. for *Pikes*, D. for *Drummes*, S. for *Serjeants*, E. for *Ensigne*, L. for *Lieutenant*, and C. for *Captaine*.

Note, if you have but three *Drummes*, then let the *Drumme* in the second *division of Pikes* bee wanting: If only two, then upon a *March*, the first betweene the third and fourth *Ranke*, of the *frons. division of Muskettiers*. The second between the third and fourth *Ranke* of the second *division of Pikes*.

Note that betweene each *Division* in *March*, there ought to be 12 *foot distance*; 6. *foot* before the *Offi-cer*, and 6. *foot* behind him.

CHAP.

Opposite: a page from a Royalist drill book, *The young Artillery man*. On the left is shown the order of march, with the captain (C) in front; the lieutenant (L) behind, pikemen (P) in the middle and musketeers (M) at either end.

Far left: a musketeer. The stand in his right hand is to support the musket when firing. From the bandolier over his shoulder hang separate charges of powder. The bullets are in the round bag. *Left:* an infantryman in armour.

Below: a commission signed by Ferdinando, Lord Fairfax, in 1643 to raise troops in the north of England.

After the battle both Rupert and Lord Forth, whom Charles had appointed as his General-in-Chief in place of Lindsey, urged the King immediately to undertake a forced march on London and compel Parliament to capitulate. He was dissuaded from doing so largely on political grounds, regarding it as a violent action which would alienate too many of his subjects. Instead on 29 October he entered Oxford, which was to remain his headquarters throughout the first civil war; then on 4 November he occupied Reading, while Rupert vainly tried to storm Windsor Castle, having already plundered Broughton Castle near Banbury, which had surrendered to the Royalists on 27 October. So it was not until nearly three weeks after Edgehill that the royal army arrived north-west of London. Meanwhile the Earl of Essex with the remnants of his army had crossed the Chiltern Hills to reach the capital a week ahead of Rupert. Essex was received as a victor and voted £5,000 as a token of esteem, but he and his officers were fully aware that they had been beaten.

On 12 November Rupert arrived at Brentford on the north side of the River Thames and, aided by a mist, surprised and occupied the town. He then advanced on Turnham Green to the east on the route to the City, but he had shot his bolt. Mainly through the efforts of John Pym and with the aid of the London trained bands, the Earl of Essex had at his command a determined army of 24,000 men. On the other side, the King's army was tired after its long march south and was short of supplies. Charles had characteristically vacillated; for he had neither earnestly pursued peace negotiations in which terms favourable to him might conceivably have been reached nor had he struck hard enough or quickly enough with a victorious army. The Parliamentarians were able to assert that the King had acted treacherously in permitting the attack on Brentford when he had in fact agreed to open negotiations. Moreover the military threat to London and the plundering which Rupert had allowed at Brentford angered and frightened people and united the City behind Pym. So the Royalists recoiled and retreated.

While King Charles was retiring to Oxford the City of London authorities volunteered to raise an additional force of cavalry, while an Ordinance imposing a property tax or assessment on the population of London and Westminster was passed by the House of Commons. A week later this assessment was extended throughout all the English counties which were under parliamentary control. At first resentment over this new imposition was expressed in the City, which had been generous enough to the cause of Parliament. But learning of Royalist successes elsewhere, the City authorities acquiesced. A new loan of £60,000 was made to Parliament; the assessment was formalized at 5 per cent on all property; and two months later Pym proposed the introduction of an excise tax (modelled on that of the Dutch) which in the end was also reluctantly accepted. What with the assessments, the excise and the sequestra-

Windsor Castle: Prince Rupert's attack in November 1642 was successfully repulsed by the Parliamentarian garrison.

tion of Royalist property wherever it could be seized Parliament accumulated a war chest sufficient to pay for the upkeep of its army and navy. Charles had to depend on voluntary loans, on contributions levied from the country round Oxford, and on the money which his Queen had succeeded in borrowing in Holland. In the long run the superiority of Parliament's financial resources was to assure the winning of the war.

During 1643 the fighting was fragmented over a number of different fronts – in Yorkshire, in East Anglia, in the west and south-west of England, and in the area round Oxford. Each side had been taken aback by its failure to achieve a striking blow in the previous autumn which might have made its enemy submit. Furthermore peace negotiations broke down because the demands put before the King by Parliament were too onerous for him. Though these negotiations continued spasmodically until March, neither side yielding an inch, fighting was already being resumed in earnest.

Dauentry

Brimidghani

The most Illustrious and High borne PRINCE RUPERT,
PRINCE ELECTOR, Second Son to FREDERICK
KING of BOHEMIA, GENERALL of the HORSE
of His MAJESTIES ARMY, KNIGHT of the Noble
Order of the GARTER.

Over the past ninety years nearly all historians have stated that in 1643 the King planned a grand strategy comprising a three-pronged thrust on London. The Earl of Newcastle, the King's General in Yorkshire, was to advance through East Anglia (hardly the quickest route to the capital); the King's army in the south-west, consisting chiefly of Cornishmen, was to move on London from the south; then the King's largest army, based on Oxford, was to launch the final assault on the capital. But there is not a shred of evidence that Charles had any such grand strategy in mind except for a story related by the Venetian representative in London to his master, the Doge, which was brought to him apparently by a servant of the King, who had formerly taught the Queen's Maids of Honour how to dance. Even that story merely stated that after the two first armies had closed upon each side of the Thames, the King aimed to 'scour the country with his cavalry', reducing London to extremities for food, and thus inducing the people to revolt against Parliament. Nothing was said about a 'final assault' on London. In fact the King had already missed his chance after the victory at Edgehill by refusing immediately to advance on the capital. He was then afraid that rather than ending the war at a blow the teeming population of the great city would turn more vehemently against him, as in fact its inhabitants did when they swarmed to Turnham Green to defy Prince Rupert. No doubt it is true that ultimately the war was likely to end with the surrender of either London or Oxford but that is no more than a military truism. The war might equally have ended with a decisive battle in any part of the kingdom.

If either side boasted a grand strategy it was not the King but Parliament. Parliament had established a Committee of Safety to co-ordinate strategy; moreover during 1643 it set about forming associations of counties to overcome the ingrained localism which caused men to refuse to fight outside their county boundaries unless they were soldiers by trade. This arrangement naturally led to the formation of other Parliamentarian armies beyond that directly under the command of the Earl of Essex. In the west Sir William Waller, who as a young man had fought in the same regiment as Essex at the beginning of the Thirty Years War in Germany and also served as a volunteer in the Venetian army, was appointed by Essex as a Major-General. Waller advanced from Winchester as far as Salisbury and then energetically swept round Dorset and Gloucestershire, seizing Tewkesbury on the River Severn. Waller's 'army' consisted of a mere 1300 men, and in a clash by the Severn with the Royalists under the command of Prince Rupert's younger brother Maurice (Ripple Field, 13 April) he met a check. But Waller remained master of the Severn Valley.

The campaign in the west began early because the winter was mild. Indeed Sir Ralph Hopton, who had also acquired military experience abroad and was to be Waller's principal opponent, had won a victory for the Royalists at Braddock Down near Liskeard

Opposite: 'The Bloody Prince', an attack on Prince Rupert after his sacking of Birmingham on 3 April 1643. Beside him runs his dog, Boy, the target of pamphleteers who celebrated his subsequent death at Marston Moor.

The standard of Sir William Waller. A shield hangs on a tree, signifying that glory is the fruit of virtue.

79

Queen Henrietta Maria, who had been in Holland raising money for the King, lands at Bridlington on 22 February 1643. She had been kept at sea for nine days by violent storms; 'Comfort yourselves, my dears,' she told her terrified attendants, 'Queens of England are never drowned.'

in Cornwall as early as 19 January. After that he persuaded the Cornishmen to march into Devon. This was followed by a truce between Cornwall and Devon, which reflected the localized character of the fighting. Meanwhile up in Yorkshire Sir Thomas Fairfax, another soldier of experience, captured Leeds for Parliament. But his force was outnumbered by that of the Earl of Newcastle. Consequently he was only able to control the West Riding. When the Queen returned from her mission to Holland she was able to land at Bridlington in the East Riding and later to join the Earl of Newcastle at York, where she stayed for three months before she made off towards Oxford to meet her husband. To skirt East Anglia (largely under parliamentary control) she went through Pontefract, Newark, Lichfield and Warwickshire. The King dispatched Prince Rupert who, using gunpowder for mining for the first time in England, captured Lichfield Cathedral, fortified and held by the Parliamentarians on 21 April, and thus prepared the way for the Queen. While Henrietta Maria was in Yorkshire the Earl of Newcastle had made considerable progress against Fairfax in the West Riding and had indeed succeeded in confining the York-

Lichfield Cathedral, scene of bitter fighting in 1643. In March it was converted into a fortress by Royalist troops, and a sharpshooter in the central tower killed the parliamentary commander, Lord Brooke. Two days later it surrendered, but in April its new occupants were in their turn besieged by Prince Rupert.

shire Parliamentarians largely to the city of Hull, which twice refused to surrender. By the beginning of July the Queen, describing herself as 'Her she-majesty, generalissima', arrived in Newark with an army of her own, and after vainly trying to capture Lincoln, eventually joined the King at Edgehill on 13 July.

Before the Queen's return the two main armies had been confronting each other in the Oxford area. The Earl of Essex, advancing from Windsor with a sizeable army, laid siege to Reading on the road to Oxford. King Charles marched from Oxford to its relief, but before he arrived the town had surrendered. The commander at Reading was court-martialled and condemned to death, but reprieved after an appeal to his father from the thirteen-year-old Prince of Wales (the future Charles II). In a somewhat leisurely way Essex moved from Reading to Thame (thirteen miles south-east of Oxford) preparatory to an attack on Oxford's defences. But Prince Rupert, after his return from his successful mission to Lichfield, crossed the Thames with an expeditionary force to surprise and outmanoeuvre Essex, whose troops still lay scattered. Near Thame Rupert engaged in a skirmish against its reinforced garrison (Chalgrove Field, 18 June) where Colonel John Hampden, the hero of the ship-money case and a close friend of John Pym, was mortally wounded. Essex then abandoned his attempt to blockade Oxford, while Rupert and his soldiers harried villages round the Chiltern Hills and unnerved the Londoners. On 26 June Essex gloomily volunteered to resign his command, but the offer was not accepted.

Elsewhere throughout the country in June and July the Royalists were equally successful. In Yorkshire Fairfax tried hard to secure the West Riding. He took and then abandoned Wakefield; on 30 June he faced a superior army commanded by the Earl of Newcastle on Adwalton Moor near Bradford, where he was severely defeated. Fairfax and his father, who, being a peer, was in nominal command, then decided to withdraw from the West Riding; Sir Thomas Fairfax brought the remnants of his exhausted cavalry to Hull where, through the courtesy of the Earl of Newcastle, he was joined by his formidable wife, a de Vere.

Meanwhile in the west of England Hopton had won a series of victories for the King. His success at the battle of Stratton in north-west Cornwall was astonishing; for he inflicted a defeat on the Parliamentarians under the Earl of Stamford with a force out-numbered by two to one and short of munitions and food, chiefly through the courage of his infantry. Hopton again advanced into Devon, from which Stamford drove him out, and thence into Gloucestershire. On 5 July Hopton faced his old friend, Waller, at Lansdown, north of Bath, and again through the heroism of the Cornish infantry defeated him in a bloody battle. Eight days later the two armies met again on Roundway Down. The Royalists were exhausted after their supreme effort at Lansdown; Hopton himself had been wounded by a gunpowder explosion and could play little part. But after the battle he brought off his men safely to Devizes in Wiltshire. Thence Prince Maurice, who was serving with Hopton, rode off to Oxford in search of reinforcements. In response to this appeal Prince Rupert himself arrived with fourteen regiments to join the western army. Together they laid siege to Bristol which they surrounded and assaulted on 26 July. After fierce fighting during which a breach was effected to the north-west of the city (at Frome Gate), the Governor surrendered. The capture of Bristol, the second most valuable port in the country, was a moment of supreme triumph for the Royalist cause. Even in eastern England where the Parliamentarians were relatively powerful they suffered rebuffs. Though the cavalry regiment raised by Colonel Oliver Cromwell distinguished itself in a skirmish at Gainsborough in Lincolnshire, the Earl of Newcastle's army advanced to the rescue from Yorkshire, and Gainsborough, Lincoln and Stamford were all abandoned to the Royalists by the first week of August.

It would appear that the time had arrived for the implementation of the King's 'grand strategy', had it ever existed, that is to say

A medal struck to celebrate the surrender of Bristol to Prince Rupert, 26 July 1643. Bristol was the second largest port in Britain, and its capture marked a high point in the Royalist struggle.

Sir Thomas Fairfax, later Baron Fairfax (1612–71), known as 'Black Tom'. In the early years of the war, when the parliamentary fortunes were at a low ebb, only he and Cromwell seemed immune to defeat. He had supreme command of the New Model Army from its creation in 1645 until 1650, and won the praise of Milton in a famous sonnet: 'Fairfax! whose name in arms through Europe rings ... Thy firm unshaken virtue ever brings Victory home ...'

converging advances upon London. On the contrary it was resolved at Oxford, against the advice of Rupert, to send the main army to capture the city of Gloucester. With Gloucester and Bristol in Royalist hands, communication between Oxford and Wales would be fully opened – a desirable position, for it was in Wales that the population was most loyal to the King. Parliament had been distressed by the series of setbacks everywhere except in East Anglia, where Oliver Cromwell was winning his reputation as a commander and had linked up with Fairfax who was later to become his superior officer; the extremists blamed the Earl of Essex for these failures and wanted William Waller to take over the command. John Pym laboured for a compromise. He managed to reconcile Essex and Waller, who did not love one another; and a new army was raised, principally in the City of London, to serve under Waller in the west. In the east an Eastern Association army under the Earl of Manchester was also virtually independent of Essex. At the same time negotiations continued between the English Parliament and leading Scots

Sir Edward Massey (1619–74), parliamentary Governor of Gloucester during the siege from 10 August to 5 September 1643, when it was relieved by an army under Essex. 'A city assailed by man but saved by God' was inscribed over one of the gates.

Lucius Cary, Viscount Falkland (c. 1610–43), depressed by the tragedy of the civil war, virtually committed suicide at the battle of Newbury on 20 September 1643. 'My Lord Falkland,' wrote Sir John Byron, 'more gallantly than advisedly, spurred his horse through the gap, where both he and his horse were immediately killed.'

for a military alliance. An approach had reached Westminster from the Marquis of Argyll, a saturnine and extremely pious Presbyterian, who feared lest Scotland might be invaded by the Irish and the northern English Royalists. Pym sent a deputation to Edinburgh, led by Sir Henry Vane, who had been highly critical of the Earl of Essex and who, not being himself a Presbyterian, was likely to protect the independence of other English Puritans.

The King arrived at Gloucester on 10 August. He set about a formal siege with cannon and attempts at mining. Prince Rupert's advice to take the town by assault, as at Bristol, was rejected on the ground that it would be too costly in human lives. But the young Governor, Edward Massey, defiantly resisted and managed to revictual the city. Rescue was put in hand at Westminster. The army under the Earl of Essex was reinforced by six regiments of the London trained bands with enough bread, cheese and beer to last it a week. On 5 September the Parliamentarian army reached the Severn and fired a salute to notify Massey that a relieving force had arrived. Regretfully the King withdrew his army, but Rupert was determined to bar Essex's way back to London, aiming to win the war for his side by a big battle.

For nearly a fortnight Essex managed to avoid contact with the Royalist army. Instead of returning by the same route on which he came (via Aylesbury and Stow-in-the-Wold) he moved after a feint into Worcestershire making for Swindon (via Cirencester and Cricklade) and thence Hungerford, Newbury and Reading, all in Berkshire. Rupert's cavalry engaged the left flank of Essex's army (at Aldbourne Chase, north-west of Hungerford) on 18 September, but were driven off. Essex then decided to put the River Kennet, which runs through Newbury, between him and the Royalists; he approached the town of Newbury on 19 September, but two hours earlier Rupert had succeeded in inserting his forces between the Parliamentarians and London. Charles I slept comfortably in Newbury that night after surprising Essex's quartermasters who were arranging billets there. To get home safely Essex now had to fight his way through. He deployed his left wing over which Major-General Skippon took command a mile south-west of Newbury while the right wing, which Essex commanded personally, stretched down to a river called the Enbrook, thus guarding against an out-flanking movement from the south. The King's army, over-confident, deployed slowly. For some reason or other a body of horse sent to occupy Wash Common plateau on its right centre withdrew before the battle began. Skippon, an old soldier, was also able to seize what was called 'Round Hill' (north of Wash Common) with infantry, thus threatening the south of the Royalist positions. Cannon was mounted on Round Hill where it could command the whole of the plain before Newbury while the Royalist cannon was placed to the east of it. Nevertheless the Earl of Essex is said to have told his soldiers that the enemy had all the advantages, 'the Hill, the

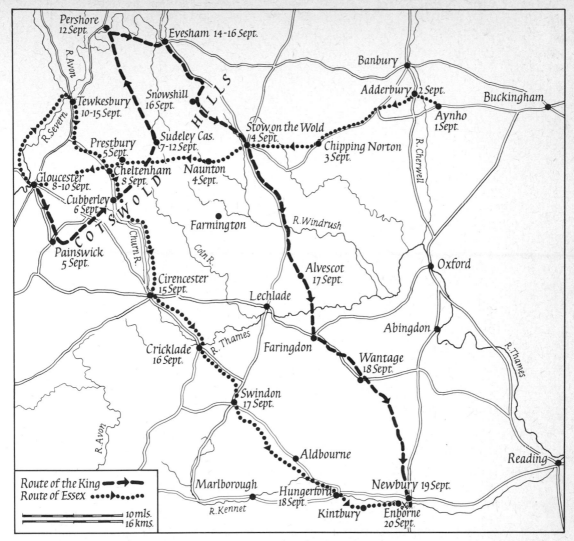

A map showing the area covered by the armies of the King and the Earl of Essex in September 1643, culminating in the first battle of Newbury.

Town, Hedges, Lane and River'. Hedges certainly lay between the two lines, but the town of Newbury was Parliamentarian in sympathy while Skippon's infantry held Round Hill.

The Parliamentarians took the offensive, for the Royalists felt they could afford to fight defensively. The battle began at seven o'clock in the morning of 20 September. On both wings the Royalist cavalry was at first victorious. But the infantry in the Parliamentarian centre stood firm. On the left foot soldiers were able to hold up the enemy cavalry in enclosed country, while in the centre Skippon called up his reserves from the London trained bands. There the pikemen aided by cannon-fire on Round Hill finally brought two Royalist cavalry regiments commanded by Sir John Byron to a standstill. Here the contest took place among the hedgerows where the cavalry were at a disadvantage: in trying to penetrate them Lord Falkland, Charles I's Secretary of State and one of the most honourable among the Royalists, was killed; a memorial marks the spot near which he died.

Altogether the battle lasted twelve hours. The King then held a council of war; Rupert and Byron wanted to fight on, but on being informed that the gunpowder was almost exhausted, Charles ordered withdrawal to Oxford. Essex's army got back safely to London by way of Reading on 25 September. According to Lord Clarendon's history, 'The Earl of Essex was received in London with all imaginable demonstrations of affection and reverence, public and solemn thanksgiving was appointed for his victory . . . it may well be reckoned amongst the most soldierly actions of this unhappy war.' A modern military historian has written that the campaign of Gloucester and the first battle of Newbury stamp Essex as one of the greatest commanders of the civil war. It certainly rehabilitated him in the minds of the Parliamentarians after the misadventures during the summer. Three years later in an elegy Essex had the credit:

> And you know the gain at Newberry!
> Seeing the General, how undauntedly
> He then encouraged you for England's right!
> When Royal forces fled, he stood the fight!

Essex's victory at the first battle of Newbury was a crucial event in the civil war, though its significance is sometimes glossed over in comparison with the later battles at Marston Moor and Naseby. It is also of interest because though there was flat and open land around Newbury the fight was concentrated in enclosed country with hedges interspersed by narrow lanes. The size of the two armies was about equal but the Royalists were much stronger in cavalry. In this hilly area of hedges and trees, however, the cavalry was of little value as it was held off by pikemen and, to a lesser extent, by musketeers. It was the only contest in the civil wars (apart from Preston) where the cavalry did not prove to be the queen of the battle. Here too artillery played some part: fifteen-pound and twenty-pound cannon balls have been discovered on the site.

The Parliamentarians, who were in many ways handicapped, being surprised and cut off from their base, fought heroically, the London militiamen in particular distinguishing themselves. The Royalists after their earlier victories may have underestimated their opponents. Yet it was their finest chance to win the war at a blow; for had the army under Essex been destroyed, the capital might have surrendered. As it was, the Parliamentarian triumph at Newbury was the turning-point in the first civil war.

Chapter Five

THE WAR WIDENS 1644

The first battle of Newbury made it clear to both sides that the war was going to last a long time, just as the earlier failure of the negotiations at Oxford, when the King had firmly refused to disband his forces as a preliminary to negotiations, showed that a compromise was impossible. During the last months of his life John Pym (who was to die of cancer in December 1643) used his diplomatic gifts to resume the search for an alliance with the Scots; he also helped to plan the formation of new armies in England which were in effect to be independent of the Commander-in-Chief. On 7 August Commissioners from the Parliament at Westminster had arrived in Leith, including Sir Henry Vane with the Congregational minister Philip Nye as his adviser, and after ten days a Solemn League and Covenant was drawn up comprising the terms for a Christian *entente* between the kingdoms of England and Scotland. The English were seeking military aid, the Scots religious conformity.

The Solemn League and Covenant of 1643 has to be sharply distinguished from the National Covenant embraced earlier by the Scots when they repudiated King Charles I's interference with the Kirk in 1638. By the Solemn League 'noblemen, barons, knights, gentlemen, citizens, burgesses, ministers of the Gospel and commons of all sorts in the kingdoms of England, Scotland and Ireland . . . living under one King and being of the reformed religion' swore to preserve the Church of Scotland and to reform the religion of England and Ireland 'according to the word of God and the example of the best reformed Churches'. The third clause of the League laid it down that they should all 'endeavour with their lives and estates' to protect 'the rights and liberties of parliaments'. The final version of the League was accepted at a meeting in St Margaret's Church, Westminster (then called 'Margaret's' so as not to offend the susceptibilities of the Puritans) on 25 September. It had already been agreed to by-pass the remnants of the House of Lords. Those who swore to the Solemn League included members not only of the House of Commons but also of the Assembly of Divines which had

Ier.50.5. Come let us joyn our selves to the Lord

in a perpetuall Covenant that shall not be forgotten.

1 6   a Solemn   4 3
LEAGUE AND COVENANT,
for Reformation, and defence of Religion, the Honour and happinesse of the king, and the Peace and safety of the three Kingdoms of **ENGLAND, SCOTLAND, and IRELAND.**

WE Noblemen, Barons, knights, Gentlemen, Citizens, Burgesses, Ministers of the Gospel, and Commons of all sorts in the Kingdomes of England, Scotland, and Ireland, by the Providence of God, living under one King, and being of one reformed Religion, having before our eyes the Glory of God, and the advancement of the kingdome of our Lord and Saviour Iesus Christ, the Honour and happinesse of the Kings Maiesty and his posterity, and the true publique Liberty, Safety, and Peace of the Kingdomes, wherein every ones private Condition is included, and calling to minde the treacherous and Bloody Plots, Conspiracies, Attempts, and Practices of the Enemies of God, against the true Religion, and professors thereof in all places, especially in these three kingdoms ever since the Reformation of Religion, and how much their rage, power and presumption, are of late, and at this time increased and exercised, whereof the deplorable state of the Church and kingdom of Ireland, the distressed estate of the Church and kingdom of England, and the dangerous state of the Church and kingdom of Scotland, are present and publique Testimonies: We have now at last, after other meanes of Supplication, Remonstrance, Protestations, and Sufferings, for the preservation of our selves and our Religion, from utter Ruine and Destruction, according to the commendable practice of these Kingdomes in former times, and the Example of Gods people in other Nations; After mature deliberation, resolved and determined to enter into a mutuall and solemn League and Covenant: Wherein we all subscribe, and each one of us for himself, with our hands lifted up to the most high God, do sweare;

I will purge out from among you the Rebels, & them that trangresse against me.

I will bring them forth out of the Countrey where they Soiourne, Ezekiel. 20.38.PAGE

IV. We shall also with all faithfulnesse endeavour the discovery of all such as have beene, or shall be Incendiaries, Malignants, or evill Instruments, by hindering the Reformation of Religion, dividing the king from his people, or one of the kingdoms from another, or making any Faction or parties amongst the people, contrary to this league & Covenant that they may be brought to publick triall, and receive condigne punishmet, as the degree of their offences shall require or deserve, or the supreä Iudicatories of both kingdoms respectively, or others having power from them for that effect, shall iudge covement.

A Malignant   A Preist

I. That we shall sincerely, really and constantly, through the Grace of God, endeavour in our severall places and callings, the preservation of the Reformed Religion in the Church of Scotland, in Doctrine, Worship, Discipline & Government, against our comon Enemies, the reformation of Religion in the kingdomes of England and Ireland, in Doctrine, Worship, Discipline and Government, according to the Word of God, and the Example of the best Reformed Churches, And shall indeavour to bring the Churches of God in the three kingdoms, to the neerest coniunction and Uniformity in Religion, Confession of Faith, Form of Church government, Directory for Worship and Catechising: That we and our posterity after us may as Brethren, live in Faith and Love, and the Lord may delight to dwell in the midest of us.

Thou hast avouched ye Lorde this day to be thy God and to walke in his wayes &c to keepe his Statutes whose Commandements he his Iudgements &c to harken to his voyce. And the Lord hath avouched thee this day to be his peculiar people & to make thee high above all nations, in praise in name & in honour. Deutero: 26: 17: 18:

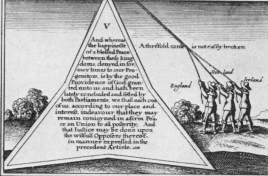

V

And whereas the happinesse of a blessed Peace between these kingdoms, denyed in former times to our Progenitors, is by the good Providence of God granted unto us, and hath beene lately concluded and setled by both Parliaments, we shall each one of us, according to our place and interest, indeavour that they may remain conioyned in a firm Peace an Union to all posterity; And that Iustice may be done upon the wilfull Opposers thereof, in manner expressed in the precedent Article.

A threefold corde is not easily broken

Scotland   England   Ireland

II. That we shall in like manner, without respect of persons, indeavour the extirpation of Popery, Prelacie, (that is Church government, by Arch-Bishops, Bishops, their Chancellors and Comissaries, Deans, Deans and Chapters, Archdeacons, & all other Ecclesiasticall Officers depending on that Hierarchy) Superstition, Heresie, Schisme, Prophanenesse, and whatsoever shall be found to be contrary to sound Doctrine, and the power of Godlinesse: lest we partake in other mens sins, and therby be in danger to receive of their plagues, and that the Lord may be one, and his Name one in the three kingdoms.

Every plant which my heavenly Father hath not planted shall be rooted out. Math. 15.

Coristers   Singing men   Deanes   Bishop

VI. We shall also according to our places & callings in this common cause of Religion, Liberty and Peace of the kingdoms, assist and defend all those that enter into this League and Covenant, in the maintaiñg & pursuing thereof, and shall not suffer our selves directly or indirectly by whatsoever combination, persuasion or teror to be devided & withdrawn from this blessed Uniõ & coniunction, whether to make defection to the contrary part, or to give our selves to a detestable indifferency or neutrality in this cause which so much cõcerneth the glory of God, the good of the kingdoms, and honour of the King; but shall all the dayes of our lives, zealously and constantly continue therein, against all opposition, and promote the same according to our power, against all Lets and impediments whatsoever, an what we are not able our selves to suppresse or overcome, we shall reveale and make known, that it may be timely prevented or removed: All which we shall do as in the sight of God.

And his heart shall be against the holy Covenant. Dan. 11. 28

III. We shall with the same sincerity, reality and constancy, in our severall Vocations, endeavour with our estates and lives, mutually to preserve the Rights and Priviledges of the Parliaments, and the Liberties of the kingdomes, and to preserve and defend the kings Maiesties person and authority in the preservation and defence of the true Religion, and Liberties of the kingdomes, that the World may beare witnesse with our consciences of our Loyaltie, and that we have no thoughts or intentions to diminish his Maiesties iust power and greatnesse.

The Lord will Create upon every dwelling place of Mount Sion, & upon her Assemblies

a Cloud and smoke by day and a shining of a flaming Fire by night, for upon all the glory shall be a defence, Isaiah 4. 5.

House of Lords   House of Commons

Also to be had by Thomas Ienner at ye Exchange

And because these kingdoms are guilty of many sins & provocations against God, & his Son Iesus Christ, as is too manifest by our present distresses and dangers the fruits thereof; We professe and declare before God and the world, our unfayned desire to be humbled for our, &c for the sins of these kingdoms especially, that we have not as we ought, valued the inestimable benefit of the Gospel, that we have not laboured for the purity and power thereof, and that we have not endeavoured to receive Christ in our hearts, not to walk worthy of him in our lives, which are the causes of other sins and transgressions, so much abounding amongst us; And our true and unfayned purpose desire, and endeavour for our selves, and all others under our power and charge, both in publick and in private, in all duties we owe to God and man, to amend our lives, and each one to go before another in the Example of a reall Reformation, that the Lord may turne away his wrath, and heavy indignation, and establish these Churches and kingdoms in truth and peace. And this Covenant we make in the presence of almighty God, the Searcher of all hearts, with a true intention to performe the same, as we shall answer at that great day when the secrets of all hearts shall be disclosed: Most humbly beseeching the Lord to strengthen us by his Holy Spirit for this end, and to blesse our desires and procedings with such successe, as may be deliverance and safety to his people, & encouragement to other Christian Churches groaning under or in danger of the yoake of Anti-christian Tyranny, to ioyne in the same, or like Association and Covenant, to the glory of God, the enlargement of the kingedo of Iesus Christ, and the peace and tranquility of Christiä kingdoms & Commonwealths.

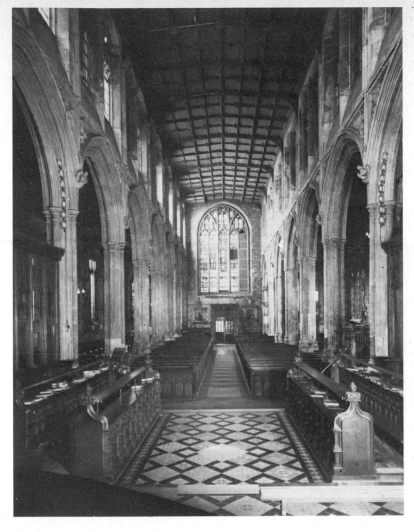

The Solemn League and Covenant, accepted at a meeting in St Margaret's Church, Westminster (*left*) on 25 September 1643, made religious concessions to the Scots in return for their military aid. Its six points, set out with illustrations in an etching by Hollar (*opposite*), covered the furthering of Presbyterianism and religious reform (I and II), a guarantee to preserve Parliament and the King (III), the suppression of religious and political trouble-makers (IV), the preservation of the union of the kingdoms of England, Scotland and Ireland (V), and a pledge of mutual support and commitment to the League (VI).

been constituted on 1 July to advise Parliament about religious reforms. Parliament had already abolished bishops and confiscated their lands, but Philip Nye, who was invited to open the proceedings on the grave occasion, was careful to point out that they were not committed to imitate the precise organization of the Scottish Kirk. That proviso was to be the source of future arguments. But Pym had got what he wanted, a military alliance. To pay for the entry of a Scottish army into England a large loan had first to be raised in the City of London, for the English Parliament undertook to pay the entire cost of a Scots army of 21,000 men, which on 19 January 1644 began its march south.

James Graham, Earl of Montrose, a sincere Calvinist who was nevertheless romantically loyal to his King, had warned Queen Henrietta Maria when she was in York and later King Charles when

Two servants of Charles I, alike in their loyalty, unlike in their fates. *Above:* the Marquis of Montrose (1612–50), Captain-General in Scotland. *Above right:* the Marquis of Ormonde (1610–88), Lord Lieutenant of Ireland. After Charles I's death Montrose returned to Scotland to try and raise the clans against Parliament, but was captured and executed, aged thirty-eight. Ormonde, after attempting to hold Ireland against Cromwell, withdrew to France and lived to enjoy a dukedom under Charles II.

he was outside Gloucester that a Scottish invasion of northern England was imminent. The King was reluctant to believe that the Scots would not remain loyal to him, especially after the conciliatory gestures he had made towards them when he visited Edinburgh in the summer of 1641. But he himself was already seeking help from Ireland. He had ordered his Lord-Lieutenant, the Marquis of Ormonde, to arrange a cessation of hostilities with the rebel Irish, which was concluded on 15 September 1643, in order that English soldiers in the Irish garrison might be brought over to fight on the Royalist side in England. Troops from Munster and Leinster began to arrive in November. Some of them were intended for the defence of Chester (the main staging point from Ireland) and others to reinforce Hopton in the south. When Charles at last recognized the genuineness of the military danger from Scotland, he appointed Montrose, who was an experienced soldier, as his Captain-General there. Montrose held out hopes that with his own kinsmen and servants and with troops landed on the west coast of Scotland from Ireland he could distract the Scottish expeditionary army from its rear after it had entered northern England and oblige it to come back home.

In February 1643, a fortnight after Montrose's appointment, a Committee of Both Kingdoms including peers like the Earls of Essex

Within the illustration:

PAINTED GLASS
IN A
WINDOW
OF
FARNDON CHURCH

Containing Portraits
of Cheshire Gentlemen
who attended K. Charles I.
at the Siege of Chester.

From a Drawing contributed by
the very Rev.ᵈ Hugh Cholmondeley
Dean of Chester.

A painted glass window commemorating members of the King's army at Chester. As the main staging point from Ireland it was a key town, and its defence was a vital issue for the Royalists throughout the first civil war (*see* p. 128).

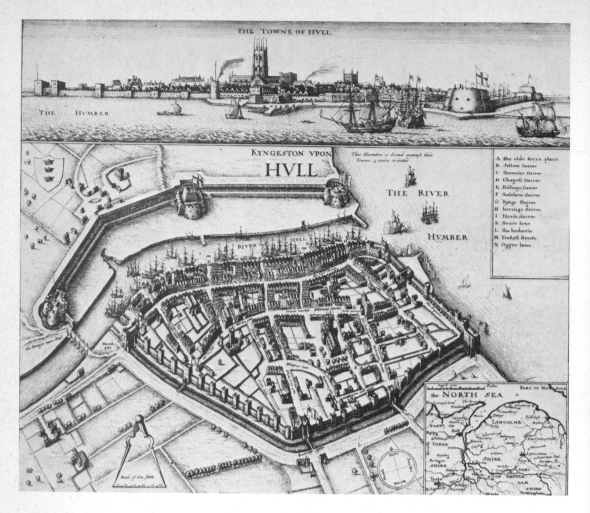

Hull, where a Parliamentarian army under Sir Thomas Fairfax was besieged from 2 September until 12 October 1643. At one point Cromwell entered the town by crossing the Humber from Lincolnshire and helped to evacuate Fairfax's cavalry.

and Warwick, members of parliament like Sir Henry Vane and Oliver Cromwell, and four Scottish representatives was formed to concert the strategy of the war. It was an unwieldy body of twenty-five members, and as its experts were usually away on duty in the field its decisions were not always wise nor realistic. Here the King as an unchallenged authority remained at an advantage in the direction of the war from his side. By now the English Parliament had formed two new armies, that of the Eastern Association (Essex, Suffolk, Norfolk, Cambridgeshire, Huntingdonshire and Lincolnshire) under the command of the Earl of Manchester and that of a South-Eastern Association (Sussex, Surrey, Hampshire and Kent) under the able Sir William Waller, which naturally created jealousies. By way of compensation at the beginning of December 1643 a vote was agreed upon to recruit the returned army of the Earl of Essex, bringing it back to a strength of 14,000 men, which was what it had been before the London trained bands were withdrawn from it after the Newbury campaign.

Charlotte de la Trémoille, Countess of Derby (1599–1664), who twice conducted the defence of Lathom House, Lancashire, against Parliament. In the spring of 1644 after four months of siege she was relieved by Prince Rupert, but a year later, in December 1645, after another long siege she was compelled to surrender.

The course of the war since that battle had favoured neither side. On the one hand, the city of Reading had been abandoned by the Parliamentarians and Prince Maurice had taken the port of Dartmouth in Devon. For a time too Winchester in Hampshire and Arundel in Sussex came under Royalist control. On the other hand, in October the Earl of Essex had taken Newport Pagnell in Buckinghamshire, a strategic point on the route between Yorkshire and London. The Earl of Newcastle was soon obliged to raise the siege of Hull, which he had begun in early September. During the siege Sir Thomas Fairfax – 'Black Tom', as he was called – a taciturn and efficient officer, had brought the cavalry not needed in Hull across the Humber to join up with Manchester's army in Lincolnshire. He and Colonel Cromwell – 'Old Noll' – soon to become Manchester's second-in-command, together defeated the Royalists in a cavalry fight at Winceby on 11 October. As a consequence Lincoln was regained for Parliament. Finally Fairfax in an inspired march across England in mid-winter confronted a Royalist force besieging Nantwich, the last Parliamentarian stronghold in Cheshire, which he defeated though the Royalist commander, Lord Byron, had been reinforced by regiments from Ireland (25 January 1644). Among the many prisoners taken was Colonel George Monck, a professional soldier who had seen Charles I and offered him his services as a volunteer, having himself recently returned from a command in Ireland. Fairfax then sat down to reduce the last Royalist stronghold in Lancashire, Lathom House, whose defence was conducted by a middle-aged Frenchwoman, the Countess of Derby.

Thus by the spring of 1644 when hostilities were resumed in earnest England was divided from the military point of view almost equally between the Roundheads, as the Parliamentarians were inappropriately nicknamed (most of the officers were gentlemen who wore their hair long), and the Cavaliers, neither side having been able materially to push back their lines. For example, the Parliamentarians under Waller retook Arundel in Sussex and repulsed the Royalists at the battle of Cheriton in Hampshire (29 March), but in Nottinghamshire they were still frustrated in their efforts to occupy the key town of Newark, which was relieved by Prince Rupert on 21 March. The arrival of the Scottish army altered the whole situation. The Earl of Newcastle ceased to have a firm hold on north-eastern England. By 20 April the Scots had safely linked up with Fairfax, returned from his successful mission to Cheshire and Lancashire, and together they laid siege to the ancient northern capital of York.

The entry of the large Scottish army into Northumberland left the Marquis of Newcastle, as he now was, with no alternative but to reinforce the garrison of the town from which he had taken his title and then, adopting delaying tactics, fall back slowly through County Durham to his stronghold at York. But in April his difficulties were increased when Sir Thomas Fairfax, flushed with his victory at Nantwich, returned to the West Riding of Yorkshire and joined his father, who came from Hull to meet him, at Selby. Learning that the Fairfaxes were preparing to meet up with the Scots near Durham, Lord Bellasis, the temporary commander at York, bravely set out to prevent this, but was comprehensively defeated by Thomas Fairfax (who was his cousin), losing all his officers and 2,000 of his men. When Newcastle learned of the disaster, he gave up his intention of confronting the Scots at Durham and hastened to shut himself up in York where he had some 4,500 infantry and 3,000 cavalry. While Fairfax, now in command of almost the whole of Yorkshire, was meeting Alexander Leslie, Earl of Leven, the Commander-in-Chief of the Scots army, Newcastle wrote to the King in alarm, saying that the enemy 'have already put themselves in such a posture as will soon ruin us, being at York unless there is some speedy course taken to give us relief'.

The situation was, however, not one of immediate danger. York was a strongly fortified city with thick stone walls three and a half miles in circumference which dated back to the Middle Ages. It contained an inner and outer moat and was protected by half a dozen gun emplacements on small forts. Supplies of food and munitions were sufficient to last the garrison for some weeks; on 22 April Newcastle decided to let most of his cavalry depart to join the King in the Midlands; he kept only 300 horse in the city. Thus the strain on his supplies was considerably diminished.

Although the Scots and the army of the Fairfaxes took up siege positions the day before, these were too few to carry out a complete blockade; so for some time Newcastle was able to send out foraging parties into the area north of the city. The consequence was that

Prospect of
NEWARKE
from Hawton way

Fairfax decided to ride over to the Earl of Manchester, whose army had captured Lincoln on 6 May (the town had changed hands more than once) to invite him to take part in the siege. Manchester accepted the invitation and reached York in a leisurely way during the first week of June. The three besieging armies were now able more or less to complete the encirclement and investment of the city. Manchester's troops covered the north, the Scots the west and the south, and Fairfax the east. To link up his forces with those of the Scots to his west Manchester had a bridge of boats constructed across the River Ouse at the suburb of Poppleton. What the three commanders had in mind was to starve the city into surrender if it could not be taken by direct assault. The artillery of those days was insufficiently powerful seriously to breach the thick walls; the only hope was mining. Cavalry patrolled the suburbs to prevent forays by the garrison. Both sides cannonaded each other from time to time without doing much damage. The Marquis of Newcastle had no intention of surrendering easily; he trusted the King to send a relieving force; meanwhile he was content to offer to treat with the enemy in the hope of gaining time.

After the parleys ended without result, the most dramatic event in the siege took place. Since Manchester's arrival while the city had been closely beleaguered tunnels had been built from the northern side with the aim of springing two mines, one under one of the city gates, the other under one of the four towers of St Mary's Manor, a large house which had been the headquarters of the Lord President of the North in the days of the rule of Viscount Strafford. The mine under St Mary's was exploded on the morning of Trinity Sunday (16 June) apparently by the order of Major-General Laurence Crawford, who commanded the infantry in the army of the Earl

The Royalist town of Newark, in Nottinghamshire, long defied the attacks of parliamentary armies. Prince Rupert came to its rescue in March 1644, defeating the besiegers and capturing a vast store of artillery and supplies.

The walled city of York, besieged by the Parliamentarians in the spring and summer of 1644. On the extreme left (numbered 3) is St Mary's Manor, which was damaged by a mine on 16 June, though without effecting a breach. The siege was raised on 1 July.

of Manchester (Oliver Cromwell commanded the cavalry). Whether Manchester knew of his subordinate's intention or not is obscure. But what is certain is that neither of the other generals was informed of the plan. No doubt the Presbyterian Crawford thought it an excellent time to assault the city while many of the officers of the garrison were attending Anglican service in the Cathedral. The tower or part of it was duly blown up and a battery breached a hole in the wall near by. Crawford gallantly led his men into the breach, aiming to take the manor-house by storm, but many of the garrison troops were able to concentrate against him and he lost 300 out of 600 of his soldiers. It was suggested afterwards that if the other generals had been notified about the attempt they could have created diversions. As it was, the besiegers were dispirited, illness was rife among the soldiers, and rumours that Prince Rupert was on his way with a big army produced, apart from a sally or two, a fortnight of inaction.

Meanwhile what had been happening elsewhere? The Parliamentarians had made an all-out effort at the outset of the 1644 campaign. Besides the Scots, they had four armies in the field. The original intention had been that the armies of the Earl of Essex and

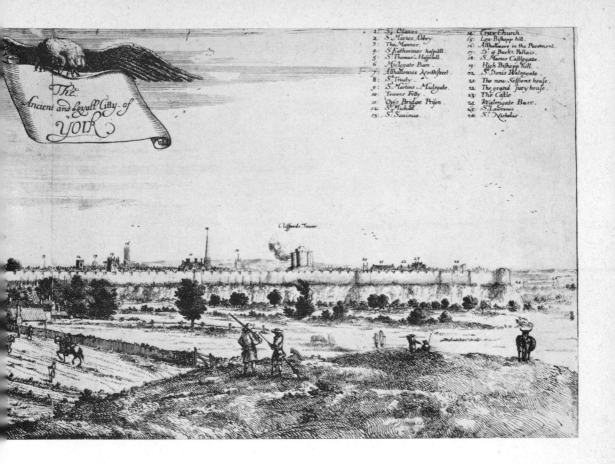

<table>
<tr><td>1.</td><td>St Olaves.</td><td>14.</td><td>Crux Church.</td></tr>
</table>

1. St Olaves.
2. St Maries Abbey.
3. The Mannor.
4. St Katherines hospitall.
5. St Thomas's Hospitall.
6. Miclegate Barr.
7. Allhallowes Northstreet.
8. St Trinity.
9. St Martins Miclegate.
10. Towers Folly.
11. Ou^{se} Bridge Prison.
12. St Michel.
13. St Saviours.

14. Crux Church.
15. Low Bishopp hill.
16. Allhallowes in the Pavement.
17. D. of Bucks Pallais.
18. St Maries Castlegate.
19. High Bishopp hill.
20. St Denis Walmgate.
21. The new Sessions house.
22. The grand Jury house.
23. The Castle.
24. Walmgate Barr.
25. St Lawrence.
26. St Nicholas.

Sir William Waller should meet at Aylesbury in Buckinghamshire and move against the King's base at Oxford. Eventually they met at Reading (which the Royalists in turn had abandoned) in the middle of May. By the end of the month Essex had occupied first Abingdon and then Islip, both close to Oxford, while Waller aimed to cut off the King from his adherents in the west. Charles I was obliged by this pressure to move out of Oxford into Worcestershire, having allowed Prince Rupert with the bulk of his forces to go north to the rescue of York. But the trouble was that the two Parliamentarian generals, as has been noted, did not get along happily together. Essex was jealous of Waller, who was probably the more capable of the two. He therefore decided to leave Waller to shadow the King, while he himself marched to the west of England. His immediate objective was to relieve the port of Lyme in Dorset, which was being besieged by Prince Maurice with a small force; Essex's argument was that if he could crush Royalism in the south-west of England, he would deprive the King of his principal source of supplies and thus shorten the war. He was also afraid that Lord Hopton would join Prince Maurice and recruit an entirely new western army for the Royalist side. The Committee of Both Kingdoms was dismayed by the decision to break up the combined army which was intended to overthrow the King and thus cease to be a threat to Oxford. But what could the Committee do? Most of the members were civilians, for officers like Manchester and Cromwell were engaged elsewhere. If the Commander-in-Chief chose to advance into the west, who were they to gainsay his considered judgment? The Earl of Essex adopted the attitude that earlier directives had instructed 'him to relieve Lyme and that it was his responsibility to give orders to his own Major-General, that is to say Waller. Essex also took care not to inform the Committee of his intentions until he was well on his way in the middle of June. Waller, left to deal with the King, was defeated at the battle of Cropredy Bridge. Cropredy Bridge lay across the River Cherwell not far from Banbury. The two forces (neither consisting of more than 3,000 men) had been moving north in parallel lines on either side of the river. The King's army was strung out in three bodies. Waller, who had seized the bridge, thrust two contingents across the river, one over the bridge, another at a ford a mile farther south, but they were separately defeated and when his infantry tried to hold the ford, because they were pikemen – their musketeers having separated from them – they were mown down and fled. Waller withdrew his small army to higher ground

Hanwell Castle, near Banbury in Oxfordshire, where Waller encamped the day before the battle of Cropredy Bridge, 29 June 1644. The castle was later slighted, but the central tower survived as part of a farm-house.

west of the Cherwell where the Royalists could scarcely hope to attack them effectively. Instead of an attack he received an engaging letter from a Royalist lady who had formerly been a flame of his, suggesting that he should change sides; but Waller remained true to his cause and drew off his men without further serious mishap. Casualties had been slight on either side, but Waller admitted that he had been worried by his loss of eleven guns and he left Charles at liberty to return to Oxford or to follow Essex into the west of England. The King for his part distinguished himself in this minor action.

Thus although the Royalists were outnumbered, they were not yet outmanoeuvred. For they still enjoyed the advantage of inner lines; the Parliamentarians were never sure where they would strike next. Indeed when Rupert was in Oxford early in May he had advised his master to reduce his commitments in the Oxford area by securing a number of strong points including Reading and Banbury while the King himself kept a cavalry force (in later days it would be called an army of manoeuvre) which could go to the assistance of any threatened garrison. By that means Rupert himself would be left free to advance north with the main Royalist army. His plan was accepted, but after Rupert left Oxford on 5 May the King, apparently on the advice of the old professional, Lord Forth, now created Earl of Brentford, who was slow, gouty and deaf, reduced his commitments even further by abandoning Reading once again and embodying its garrison in his own army. As it proved, the decision worked out excellently, partly because the Earl of Essex had left Waller too small a force to incommode the King, who was thus left free, like Rupert, to go wherever he wished.

After Rupert left Oxford he first made for Lancashire to recruit his strength in an area largely Royalist in sympathy. In the space of a fortnight he moved through Stockport in Cheshire and Bolton, Wigan, Liverpool and Preston in Lancashire, relieving on his way Lathom House, still indomitably held by the Countess of Derby against the parliamentary besiegers left behind by Fairfax. The Committee of Both Kingdoms was sufficiently perturbed to send Sir Henry Vane to York to urge the generals there to dispatch an expedition into Lancashire so as to regain Fairfax's earlier conquests. Though the evidence is rather flimsy, it has been thought – and this is seemingly accepted by his latest biographer – that Vane also wanted to sound the three generals besieging York about the idea that the King, once he was beaten, should be deposed and a republic estab-lished in place of the monarchy. But the generals could not be persuaded to divide or divert their armies; they took the view that Rupert would sooner or later come their way and that they then could deal with him. They were right.

On 14 June Charles I had written a letter to Rupert in which he peremptorily commanded him to march at once to the relief of York, saying 'If York be lost, I shall esteem my crown little less . . .'.

On the wall of the parish church of Cropredy hang several pieces of armour found after the battle. They include back- and breast-plates and a helmet, the armour of a pikeman. The splendid lectern in the foreground is said to have been hidden in the River Cherwell to save it from the Puritans.

A succession of historians and biographers have written glosses on this letter, which is obscurely worded. Rupert certainly interpreted it to mean that not only was he to relieve York but to 'beat the rebels' armies which were before it'. A modern military historian has averred that no staff officer today could have thought that Charles intended his nephew to fight a battle at all costs whether the siege of York had been raised or not. Yet at the time John Culpeper, the King's Chancellor of the Exchequer, observed to Charles after the letter was dispatched, 'Before God, you are undone, for upon the peremptory order, he will fight whatever comes on't.'

The commanders round York learned on 28 June that Rupert was on his way; two days later he was known to be in Knaresborough, which lies about twelve miles west of York. A council of war was held and it was decided to march out to meet him, for the generals had no wish to be caught between Rupert's relieving army and the garrison under Newcastle sallying forth from the city (in the same way and for the same reason that King Charles had resolved to raise the siege of Gloucester the year before). They therefore led their armies on to Marston Moor, four miles west of York, so as to bar any approach from Knaresborough. Their cavalry was sent ahead and the infantry followed. They could not imagine that Rupert would advance upon York in any other way, for then he would be obliged to follow a circuitous route crossing first the River Ouse, then its tributary the Swale and finally the Ouse again at Poppleton where the bridge of boats had been left in charge of a regiment of dragoons. The Prince, however, did precisely that. On 1 July his infantry made a forced march of twenty-two miles from Knaresborough, surprised the dragoons, captured the bridge of boats, and encamped at the forest of Galtres north of York. That evening the Marquis of Newcastle sent him a letter of gratitude, professing himself 'made of nothing but thankfulness and obedience'. But Rupert committed an error by not himself entering York to concert operations with the proud Marquis. Instead he dispatched his General of Horse, Lord Goring, with a message for Newcastle to come out and join him on Marston Moor. As Newcastle and his garrison had been holding out for ten weeks against a vast besieging army, they were tired and hungry. The Marquis understandably was not amused.

Both Rupert's army and the allies were up early the following morning. The allied generals had convinced themselves the night before that after the relief of York Rupert would make for the south to rejoin the King or else invade the territory of the Eastern Association south of Newark left vulnerable in the absence of Manchester's army. The three allied forces therefore began marching south in the direction of Tadcaster (ten miles south-west of York). They had got some distance and were strung out along the Tadcaster road when Sir Thomas Fairfax, commanding the Yorkshire cavalry, some 3,000 in number, spotted to his rear about 5,000 Royalist cavalry

deploying upon Marston Moor. The allied generals, who were still at Long Marston, a village to the east of the moor, were alarmed. Would the unpredictable Prince strike them from behind? They hastened to recall their vanguard which was moving on to Tadcaster and spent the rest of the morning and early afternoon drawing up their men in order of battle on the sloping land covered with rye called Marston Field, facing the moor.

By four o'clock in the afternoon the allies were all in position. At the same time Newcastle's infantry, known as the Whitecoats after the undyed woollen uniforms they wore, at last reached Marston Moor from York. It may well be that Newcastle himself had arrived earlier, relying upon his professional military adviser, Lord Eythin, to bring out the garrison. But the soldiers had proved obstreperous, demanding pay and plunder, so that it was no one's fault that they did not get on the moor until four o'clock in the afternoon. By then Rupert had already carried out the marshalling of his own army. He had taken advantage of a long and deep ditch which separated the two armies; he lined this ditch with musketeers and small 'drakes' or guns, while not far behind them he stationed the front lines of his cavalry on the flanks and his infantry in the middle. He gave orders to Lord Byron on his right wing that he must stand his ground and 'receive the charge of the enemy'. The bulk of Rupert's men had been on the alert since the early morning; they had been kicking their heels and eating their rations while waiting for the Whitecoats to arrive. After twelve hours they were naturally tired.

The precise character of Rupert's plan is not clear except that he wanted a battle, which he believed the King had ordered him to fight. But had he in fact considered attacking the Parliamentarian

'The English-man did lead the van with musket and pike' ran a popular song. Pikemen (*above*) and musketeers normally stayed close to each other for mutual protection, since muskets took an appreciable time to reload.

General Leslie.

The battle of Marston Moor, 2 July 1644. *Left*: the Scots Earl of Leven (*c.* 1580–1661), Commander-in-Chief of the allied forces. *Below left*: part of an account of the battle by a Parliamentarian officer, Sir James Lumsden, published three days later in Edinburgh.

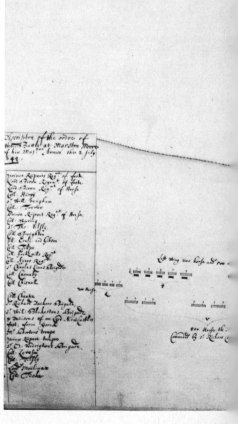

perceiving, brought up theirs, and gave us the like. This continued not long, when it was resolved wee should advance downe the hill through a great field of corne, to a ditch they had in possession, when it pleased God so to prosper, they were put from it, so that the service went on verie hote on all sides : We losing on the right Wing, and gaining on the left , they that fought stood extraordinar well to it ; whereof my Lord *Lindesays* Briggad beeing commanded by himselfe, was one. These Briggads that failyied of the Vane were presently supplied by *Cassels*, *Cowper*, *Dumfermling*, and some of *Clydisdailes* Regiment, who were on the battell, and gained what they had lost, and made themselves master of the Canon was next to them, and tooke Sir *Charles Lewcas* Leivetenant Generall of their Horse prisoner : These that ran away shew themselves most basely. I commanding the Battel, was on the head of your Lordships Regiment and *Buclenches*; but they carried themselves not so as I could have wished, neither could I prevaile with them: For these that fled, never came to charge with the enemie, but were so possest with a panatick feare , that they ran for an example to others , and no enemie following them, which gave the enemie to charge them, they intended not, & they had only the losse. These that fought, God preserved them miraculously with no losse, we have only the Lord *Dudup* prisoner , and Lievetenant Collonel *Brison* is killed , two Captaines, and some Souldiers: We have Sir *Charles Lewcas*, Generall Major *Porter* , some Collonels, and other officers, with sundrie of their chiefe Officers killed. The number killed to the enemie as is estimate, is two thousand, and above, with fifteene hundreth prisoners , twentie piece of Canon ,

Below: a plan of the battle of Marston Moor, drawn by the Royalist engineer Sir Bernard de Gomme. Across the centre runs the hedge and ditch, with the Royalist armies below it and the allied armies on the hill above (top), separated from it by 'a great field of corne' (see Lumsden's account, *opposite*). On the left, Goring's cavalry faced Fairfax's; in the centre is the infantry (shown in black), commanded on one side by Newcastle and on the other by Leven; on the right, Byron's cavalry confronted Cromwell's, which was to win the day.

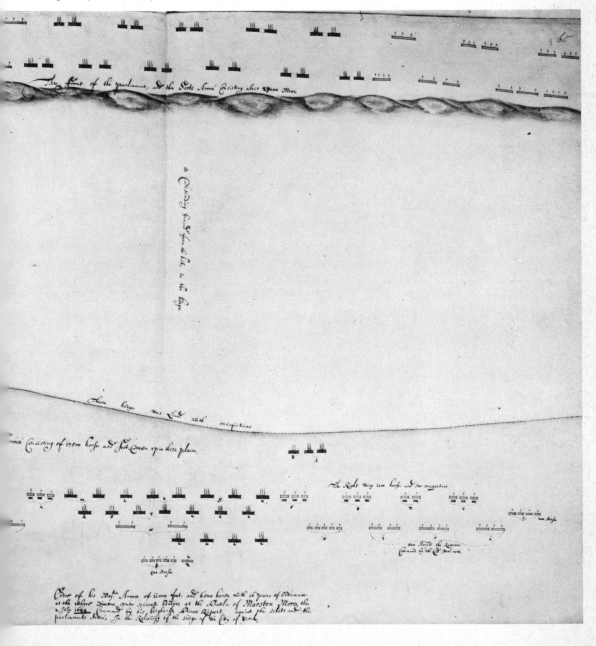

rear early in the morning? Did he want to start a set battle in the afternoon? When eventually he discussed matters with Newcastle and Eythin they both objected to fighting at all that day. Newcastle argued that left alone the allies might quarrel among themselves, while if the Royalists delayed, reinforcements might reach them from the north. Eythin criticized Rupert's lay-out of his regiments as being too far forward; he added rudely that Rupert's 'forwardness had lost them the day' in Germany six years earlier, when he had been taken prisoner at Vlotho. Rupert had then been eighteen. Now at the age of twenty-four in supreme command of the King's army he meekly offered to draw back his men, but was told abruptly that it was too late – though it is not clear why. Certainly Rupert's occupation of the ditch as his forward defensive position was unusual. Presumably his intention was to induce his enemies to attack him, hoping to catch them at a disadvantage by disrupting them before they reached his main body. But as evening drew on with nothing much happening except a crash of thunder and the fall of summer rain, the Royalists came to the conclusion that no battle was likely to start until the morrow.

However the allied Commander-in-Chief, the little old soldier, the Scots Earl of Leven, resolved to attack. A summer's night, it was said, was as long as a winter's day. It may well be that the Scots General ordered a reconnaissance before the Whitecoats arrived and assumed that the three armies vastly outnumbered the Royalists. A council of war was called. Probably neither Sir Thomas Fairfax nor Lieutenant-General Cromwell attended it since they were still absorbed in drawing up their own troops. The Earl of Manchester and Lord Fairfax were amateur soldiers and would clearly have followed Leven's advice.

Exactly how much inferior the strength of the Royalist army was is uncertain. A recent examination of new evidence suggests that they were not outnumbered by 10,000 men as has usually been stated. The Parliamentarians may have been superior in cavalry, but not so much so in infantry. And after Edgehill Rupert had reason to believe that his cavalry excelled in quality. So he was hardly being foolish when he courted battle. On both wings the cavalry faced one another; and in both cases platoons of musketeers were interspersed among the troops of mounted men after the Swedish fashion. On the Parliamentarian left Cromwell was opposed to Lord Byron and on the right Sir Thomas Fairfax faced Lord Goring. It is likely that Leven commanded the infantry on one side and Newcastle on the other. The signal for attack was given by the roar of cannon at about seven o'clock in the evening; the battle was all over two hours later when bright moonlight still permitted pursuit.

Cromwell's men charged across the ditch and routed Byron's first line. 'We came down', recorded his Scoutmaster-General, 'in the bravest order, and with the greatest resolution that ever was seen. . . . In a moment we were past the ditch into the Moor, upon

Oliver Cromwell (1599–1658), whose success at Marston Moor made his military reputation and won him the nickname of Ironside. His qualities as a cavalry leader were the reverse of Prince Rupert's – firm control, discipline and ability to maintain cohesion in battle. There are no very early portraits of Cromwell; this unfinished miniature, painted by Samuel Cooper about six years after Marston Moor, is the most vivid likeness.

equal grounds with the enemy, our men going into a running march.' After Byron's first line, charging against orders, suffered defeat, he threw in his second line and Prince Rupert himself, abandoning the general direction of the battle, came up with his reserve to check the enemy's advance. Lieutenant-General David Leslie, who with a small force of Scottish cavalry was in command of Cromwell's second line, then attacked from the flank, and soon the Royalist right wing was routed. Cromwell received a slight wound in the neck but he was able to take part in the cavalry action which won the victory. Afterwards he was there to steady and rally his troopers. Sir Thomas Fairfax, as he afterwards wrote, rode right across the battlefield to seek help, for Goring had pushed back the Yorkshire cavalry which was handicapped by having to advance along a narrow lane covered with a mass of gorse.

Together Fairfax and Cromwell first reversed the fortunes on their right wing by defeating Goring's victorious cavalry; they next attacked the Royalist infantry until then unshaken in the centre. The blood-stained Whitecoats died with their boots on, for they refused to surrender. Before that, of the three leading allied generals Leven and Lord Fairfax fled the field, believing that all was lost, while Manchester was on the point of doing the same. It has been a subject of speculation whether David Leslie was the real victor on the allied left and whether it was in fact Thomas Fairfax who was responsible for completing this remarkable triumph after the whole front appeared to have collapsed. But most contemporaries gave the credit to Oliver Cromwell, the middle-aged farmer who won his military reputation in this battle and was henceforward nicknamed Ironside. Even if the part he played is minimized, the fact remains that it was the thorough way in which he had trained his East Anglian cavalry – so much better disciplined than Rupert's – that turned the scales. As for Rupert, the mistakes he made were those of a brilliant and enthusiastic young officer. At least he rallied his shattered army and lived to fight another day; whereas the Marquis of Newcastle, the personal friend of Charles I and governor of his son, could not stomach the disgrace of defeat and left England to go into exile.

The Earl of Essex had experienced no difficulty in relieving Lyme in the middle of June. On 10 July the Parliamentarians occupied Taunton in Somerset and on 23 July Essex also relieved Plymouth in Devon. Next he crossed the River Tamar into Cornwall in pursuit of his intention to win the whole of the south-west from the King. But by then Charles himself was on Essex's heels. Essex occupied Lostwithiel, a port on the River Fowey, in order to maintain contact with the Earl of Warwick and the Parliamentarian fleet. Neither side received a warm welcome in Cornwall, which was independently minded, but the King, who was careful not to impound supplies, was the more popular. By the end of the first week in August the Royalists began to corner the army of Essex. There were in fact four Royalist armies in Devon (though the whole of them barely equalled a modern division). When Prince Maurice and Lord Hopton joined the King and Sir Richard Grenville arrived from the abandoned siege of Plymouth, the King had collected 16,000 men against 10,000 Parliamentarians, Essex having dispersed some of his troops on garrison duties. On 7 August Charles called upon Essex to surrender. When he refused, his force was methodically hemmed into a narrow strip of land stretching from Lostwithiel to the harbour of Fowey village, the Royalists taking command of the hills that dominated it and thus threatening their enemy's access to the sea. On 31 August Sir William Balfour and 2,000 Parliamentarian cavalry successfully cut their way out, escaped up the Bodmin road and arrived safely in Plymouth. After that Essex threw in the towel. 'I thought it fit', he wrote, 'to look to myself, it being a greater terror to me to be a slave to their contempts than a thousand deaths.' He got away in a fishing-boat but all his infantry surrendered. They were granted extremely lenient terms. Officers were allowed to retain their arms and the soldiers were permitted, once they reached Portsmouth or Southampton, to fight again. It was a curious

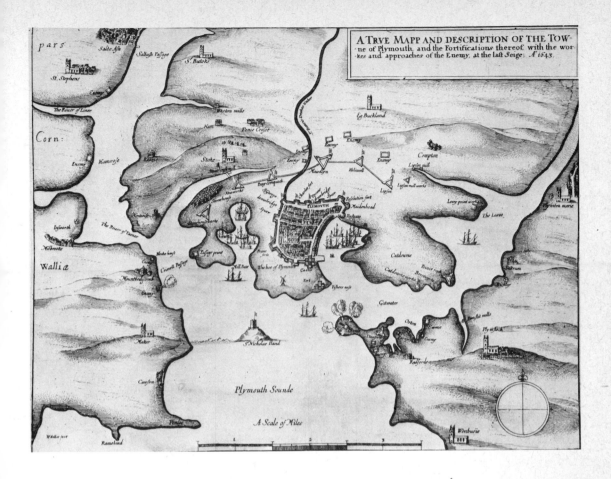

decision. But the Cornish had had enough of the Parliamentarians' depredations. The beaten foot soldiers were obliged to march without food or shelter on the way; they were stripped of their very clothes. Of the 6,000 men who left Lostwithiel on 2 September only 1,000 survived. The rest died of starvation, disease and exposure. It was one of the most terrible episodes in the first civil war.

After the battle of Marston Moor the three Parliamentarian armies had broken up; the Scots went north to besiege Newcastle upon Tyne which fell to them on 19 October. Manchester's army returned to the Eastern Association and Fairfax to Yorkshire. In the Midlands Waller was still licking his wounds after his defeat at Cropredy Bridge. Thus the House of Commons needed to take the military dispositions into account so as urgently to repair the damage done at Lostwithiel and to prevent the King's return to Oxford. The Earl of Essex was not censured for his misfortune, which he himself blamed on one of his subordinates. Instead Manchester and Waller were instructed to join up with the remnants of Essex's army. Manchester, who was dispirited and anxious to bring the war to an end by negotiation, obeyed his orders slowly and incompletely.

Plymouth was resolutely Parliamentarian and twice suffered attack by the Royalist armies, in 1643 and 1644. This map shows the line of triangular forts built some distance north of the old walls.

Shaw House, the mansion converted by the King into a fortress during the second battle of Newbury (October 1644). It stood in the centre of the Royalist line, which extended from the town of Newbury in the south-east to Donnington Castle in the north.

But the King was also moving slowly, for his army was tired, unpaid and half-starved after its long marches and exhausting campaign. It was not until 15 October that he reached Salisbury by way of Chard and Sherborne. On the 18th he left Salisbury and chased Waller out of Andover. But Waller got away to meet Manchester at Basingstoke. On 21 October Essex joined Manchester at Basing House, eight miles south-east of Newbury, which was reached by the Royalists on 22 October.

The Committee of Both Kingdoms made a pusillanimous decision about the command of the united armies: it appointed no single general to command and left it to a council of war to take charge of operations. On this council Waller was the stalwart. He declared, speaking of the Royalists at Newbury: 'Destroy this [army] and the work is ended.' Manchester was less enthusiastic, while Essex, who had caught a cold, never joined the council of war at all. The united army consisted of 19,000 men of whom 8,000 were cavalry; the King had about 10,000 men and had summoned Prince Rupert to his aid, but the Prince did not arrive until after the ensuing battle.

The second battle of Newbury was fought north of the area covered by the first battle there, but this time the Royalists again faced east. The King's army was ably deployed. The town of Newbury and the River Kennet protected its right flank. In the centre stood a large mansion called Shaw House, which was converted into a formidable strong point. The left rested on the River Lambourne, a tributary of the Kennet, while to the left rear was Donnington Castle, a small fortress which had been held by the Royalists for over a year, and south of it the village of Speen where the reserves under Prince Maurice were placed. The council of war, probably incited by Waller, resolved to divide its forces. The bulk of them were to undertake a fifteen-mile circuitous night march and then attack the enemy at Speen from the rear. Once their objective had been reached Manchester with the rest of the Parliamentarian army was to assault Shaw House, where the Royalists would presumably be weakened and distracted. Some military historians have commended the boldness of the plan. But it had its defects: first, it meant dividing the army (the great Duke of Marlborough's last words are said to have been 'Don't divide the army').

Donnington Castle, of which the gatehouse survives, had already endured a long siege in the King's cause before October 1644. During the second battle of Newbury its guns prevented the Parliamentarian success against Prince Maurice's troops from turning into victory, and Charles was able to withdraw with his army relatively intact.

Secondly, it was planned and carried out by a committee; even the attack on Speen was in the hands of four different commanders. Thirdly, it involved a long night march, one of the most difficult operations in war. Fourthly, it required cavalry to act in what was largely enclosed country. Lastly, its success depended upon a precise synchronization of attacks, which was extremely hard to achieve in the seventeenth century.

In fact though the night march and the attack were carried out successfully and the village of Speen fell to the Parliamentarians at three o'clock in the afternoon of 27 October, the Royalists, who had received warning of a coming assault on their rear, rallied and drove the enemy back. This check came at five o'clock by which time it was dark. The Earl of Manchester did not assault Shaw House with his infantry columns until about four, when he should have begun an hour earlier, and he was repulsed. The losses on both sides were relatively small. The King got away safely and was able to return later with Rupert, whom he had finally appointed as his over-all commander in place of the doddery Lord Brentford, to relieve Donnington Castle which contained cannon and valuable stores and which the Parliamentarians had been unable to capture. Manchester had preferred to secure the town of Newbury after the battle rather than to attack Donnington Castle again. A fortnight later Charles I was back in Oxford to take up his winter quarters.

The second battle of Newbury is often described as a victory by the Parliamentarians because they held the field while the King was forced to retire or retreat. But the object of the battle was to prevent the King's return to Oxford, and afterwards, because it was night and the Parliamentarian cavalry was tired, he was not pursued very far. Furthermore the Parliamentarians were unable even after the departure of the King's army to occupy Donnington Castle. Manchester's slowness in arriving and the lack of energy which he displayed in the battle aroused suspicions. After the battle he replied to a criticism by Sir Arthur Haslerig who fought there: 'Thou art a bloody fellow. God give us peace, for God does never prosper us in our victories to make them clear victories.' The defeat of the Earl of Essex at Lostwithiel and Manchester's failures – both the Earls had disobeyed orders from the Committee of Both Kingdoms – caused Parliament to realize that it must raise fresh armies and find better generals if it was to win the war.

Chapter Six

PARLIAMENT'S VICTORY 1645–1646

The campaign of 1644 ended in an atmosphere of frustration and bitterness on both sides. The King had demoted his principal military advisers and relegated two other leading officers, Lord Wilmot and Lord Percy, whom he replaced with Lord Goring and Lord Hopton, both certainly more capable commanders. Also he had had the Governor of Blechington House near Oxford, which had surrendered to Cromwell, put to death for cowardice. On the Parliamentarian side at the beginning of the New Year Sir Alexander Carew, after trial by court martial, was executed for attempting to betray Plymouth to the Royalists, while the House of Commons refused to reprieve the two Hothams, father and son, who having once defied the King, had then planned to hand over the port of Hull to Royalists. On 10 January 1645 Archbishop Laud, the victim of Puritan vindictiveness, after being condemned to death by an

The execution of Archbishop Laud, from a broadsheet of 1645. The hostile verses that accompany the engraving conclude: 'Like a blest martyre you will dye/ for churches good she riseth high/when such as you fall down.'

Ordinance of Attainder was executed for treason, which he had definitely not committed. As six days before his execution the Book of Common Prayer had been abolished in favour of a Presbyterian directory of worship, this appeared to be the end of an era for the Church of England.

Although the battle of Marston Moor had been won by the Parliamentarians and the cities of York and Newcastle had been lost by the Royalists, thus virtually placing north-east England in the hands of Parliament, these events had to some extent been compensated by the humiliation of Parliament's Commander-in-Chief at Lostwithiel and by the rebuff suffered by the united Roundhead armies at the second battle of Newbury. Moreover the Marquis of Montrose, Charles I's Captain-General in Scotland, had in August 1644 reached the verge of the Highlands and, raising an army from the clans, occupied Perth and Aberdeen in the King's name. At the beginning of February 1645 he was to defeat the Campbells, the clan of the Marquis of Argyll, the most powerful chieftain in Calvinist Scotland, at the battle of Inverlochy, though Argyll himself only watched it from his barge moored in a near-by loch in which he afterwards escaped. The only area in which the parliamentary forces had been consistently successful was East Anglia (except for the failure to capture Newark). In 1644 Lincoln had been taken by the Eastern Association army under the Earl of Manchester, Edward Montagu. Moreover Manchester's Lieutenant-General of Horse, Oliver Cromwell, had won his spurs at Marston Moor and was rightly regarded as the moving spirit in military affairs in that part of England.

The Montagus and the Cromwells were both well-established families in Huntingdonshire. They had shared the representation of the county or county town in the House of Commons over recent years. But no doubt little love was lost between them. Oliver Cromwell's rich uncle (a Royalist), ruined by extravagance, sold his estate to the Montagus while his nephew had moved away to Ely. When Oliver was a young man he had appeared before Henry Montagu, first Earl of Manchester, claiming that the mayor and aldermen of Huntingdon were in a position to filch the rights of the burgesses. Later after he had been elected a member of parliament for the city of Cambridge, he supported complaints made by Manchester's tenants against their landlord over enclosures. Cromwell was said to have been passionately angry when attending a parliamentary committee on the matter and to have accused the Chairman of partiality. Cromwell always had a hot temper, which sometimes led him into trouble. By 1644, however, he had proved himself not only a born cavalry officer but also a splendid military organizer. Again and again he asserted that 'men of a spirit' could be trained to fight as well as the Royalists and he proved his point. Insisting that a man's religion had nothing to do with his military capacity, he had criticized his colleague, Major-General Crawford,

who commanded the infantry for Manchester, of victimizing soldiers who were not, as he was, Presbyterian. Indeed Manchester had to take both his two subordinate commanders up to the Committee of Both Kingdoms in London before a reconciliation could be effected.

Cromwell, who was a vehement Puritan and resented Charles I's favouritism towards High Church bishops and clergy, was determined that the war should be won not merely to enforce constitutional reform but also to ensure the thorough refashioning of the English Church. Manchester, on the other hand, although he had been the principal critic of the King in the House of Lords before the war, had come to believe that the war must end not with victory but with reconciliation. He owed his position to his status and his wealth, but he was not a good general. He had disobeyed orders to send a contingent to Chester in August 1644, offering elaborate excuses for not doing so. Earlier he had rejected Cromwell's suggestion that he should organize an offensive against Newark. He was blamed for failing to launch the assault on Shaw House during the second battle of Newbury earlier than he did and for refusing to pursue the King after the battle was over. In the middle of November 1644 the Committee of Both Kingdoms significantly ordered him to keep his forces together and to do nothing without the approval of a council of war of which Cromwell was a member. Later in the month Cromwell in his capacity as a member of the Committee of

Edward Montagu, Earl of Manchester (1602–71), *above*, commander of the Eastern Association army, and his Lieutenant-General of Horse, Oliver Cromwell. It was largely as a result of Cromwell's criticism that Manchester lost his command in 1645 (*see* p. 115).

THE
SOULDIERS
CATECHISME:

Composed for

The Parliaments Army:

Consisting of two Parts : wherein
are chiefly taught :

1 *The Iustification* } of our Souldiers.
2 *The Qualification* }

Written for the Incouragement and In-
struction of all that have taken up Armes in
this Cause of God and his People; especially the common Souldiers.

2 Sam. 10. 12. *Be of good courage, and let us
play the men for our people, and for the Cities of our God, and the Lord do that which
seemeth him good.*

Deut. 23. 9. *When the Host goeth forth against
thine enemies, then keepe thee from every
wicked thing.*

Imprimatur. JA. CRANFORD.

Printed for J. Wright *in the* Old-Baily. 1644

Both Kingdoms and a member of parliament asserted that Manchester had been responsible for losing the battle of Newbury on the ground that he did not want to prosecute the war 'unto a full victory' because he thought that an accommodation could be reached with the King. Furthermore Cromwell blamed Manchester for preferring to retire to Newbury rather than trying to fight the King again in order to prevent the loss of Donnington Castle; and he related that when Manchester had been urged to do so on the ground that a victory at that time would have been decisive, he retorted that 'if we beat the King ninety-nine times yet he is King still, and his posterity, and we subjects still; but if the King beat us once we should be hanged and our posterity undone'. Friends of the Earl charged Cromwell with being cruel and covetous and with favouring 'common men of poor parentage' in preference to 'honest gentlemen' for recruitment to his regiment – such men were said to be 'Independents' with preaching officers and 'godly precious men' who would be sure to make a nuisance of themselves when the war ended – but Sir William Waller gave his valuable backing to Cromwell's criticisms of Manchester.

The majority in the House of Commons was impressed. Gradually it dawned on them that the failures of 1644 were principally due to the incapacity of Essex and Manchester. It was unfortunate that they both happened to be members of the attenuated House of Lords, but it could not be helped. After Cromwell had poured out his grievances he became more tactful. Observing that the blame could not be laid upon any particular commander – indeed he had made mistakes himself – he suggested that all members of parliament who held military posts should forthwith make a self-denying gesture by resigning. Thus all suspicions of corrupt practices would be contradicted; they could start again with a white sheet. A new army could be recruited with a new and blameless Commander-in-Chief. That was the right way, he believed, to win the war. Cromwell also proposed later that the Scottish army, having taken Newcastle, should be invited to come south. Naturally the House of Lords did not care for the implied aspersions on the two Earls; however the draft of the 'Self-Denying Ordinance' was amended, merely calling upon all members of parliament to resign their commands within forty days of its passing; nothing was said about their not being eligible for reappointment. After arguments stretching over four months the House of Lords was at last persuaded to agree both to the formation of what was to be known as the 'New Model Army' and to the Self-Denying Ordinance. To the general relief before the second Ordinance was passed Essex and Manchester voluntarily laid down their commissions. Sir Thomas Fairfax, who was not a member of parliament, was on Cromwell's proposal appointed the new Commander-in-Chief. He was a modest man, devoid of intrigue and a proven soldier. Harsh terms were presented to the King at a conference between representatives of the two sides held at Uxbridge

Opposite: title-page of *The Souldiers Catechisme*, designed for the use of soldiers in the Parliamentarian army 'that have taken up Armes in this Cause of God and his People'.

Sir Thomas Fairfax, Commander-in-Chief of the New Model Army, presiding over the Council of the Army in 1647, when, disgusted by its treatment at the end of the war, the army refused to obey the Parliament that had created it.

in Middlesex during the first fortnight of May 1645. They required Charles to accept Presbyterianism as the national religion of England, to allow the army and navy to be permanently controlled by Parliament and also to permit Parliament to be entirely responsible for waging war against the Irish rebels. Needless to say, these demands were rejected. So when the campaigning season opened that spring the war was vigorously resumed.

Sir Thomas Fairfax, who was to be the young Commander-in-Chief of the New Model Army (he was thirty-three) arrived in London from Yorkshire in the middle of February but it was not until April that his appointment was approved by Parliament; thereupon he departed for Windsor to see to the organization of this new force. The establishment for the New Model Army was 22,000 men, comprising eleven regiments of cavalry, twelve regiments of infantry and one regiment of dragoons, together with an artillery train. The nucleus of the cavalry was provided from what had been the Earl of Manchester's army, which had been largely trained by Cromwell. That was (apart from his political activities) Cromwell's

The uniform of a cavalry trooper in the New Model Army. Over the buff leather coat (stained with yellow ochre) is an iron back- and breastplate, crossed by the calibre belt supporting a gun at the right and the shoulder belt supporting a sword at the left. The left, or bridle, arm is shielded by an iron gauntlet. The 'pot' helmet has a protective flange at the back and a vizor above the distinctive grid in front.

only contribution to the creation of this army, which was Fairfax's responsibility. Over 8,000 men had to be pressed to join the infantry, which had not been brought up to strength when the campaign began. The infantry – musketeers and pikemen – wore red uniforms; the cavalrymen, who were paid three times as much as the infantry (two shillings a day as compared with eightpence) but were expected to provide their own horses, wore light headpieces or 'pots', armour over their back and breast and usually a buff coat of leather; their weapons were firelock pistols and swords. Because of the mixed character of the infantry the Royalists mocked at the New Model and anticipated no difficulty in crushing it.

The beginnings of the campaign of 1645 are confusing because the authorities on both sides kept on changing their minds. The King still had hopes of making the west of England into a Royalist bastion, whatever happened elsewhere. On 5 March he sent his eldest son, the future Charles II, who was not yet fifteen, to be his Captain-General in the west (with of course military and civilian advisers). The boy Prince set up his headquarters at Bristol where he

Charles, Prince of Wales, later Charles II (1630–85), became his father's Captain-General in the West in 1645. This portrait, in which he holds a commander's baton, was painted by Dobson probably to commemorate the Prince's entry into military life, when with his brother James he watched the battle of Edgehill in 1643.

soon got into all sorts of difficulties. To clear the ground in the west the independent-minded Lord Goring laid siege to Taunton on 11 March for a second time. Fairfax was duly ordered to march to the relief of Taunton at the head of his new army while Cromwell was left to harass Oxford. But it hardly needed a whole army to relieve Taunton any more than when the Earl of Essex took his army to relieve Lyme the year before. In fact Goring abandoned the siege before Fairfax could arrive, while by the time that Fairfax reached Blandford in Dorset he was recalled to deal with a threat to the Midlands. For it was known that the King's army in Oxford was being reinforced, though it was not clear where it was going to strike. Fairfax was ordered to lay siege to Oxford. But a fortnight before he began to do so, the King and Prince Rupert had left the city. Nobody knew what was their objective; the truth was that the Royalists did not know themselves.

In fact each side had divided its forces. The Royalists at least had plans for strengthening their main army by recalling Goring from the west. But what to do with it? Montrose's victory at Inverlochy and his later defeat of a Covenanter army at Auldearn, a village near Nairn in northern Scotland, in the first week of May, had two consequences. First, they weakened the Scottish army in England, for Leven sent back eight regiments to help fight Montrose. Secondly, Prince Rupert urged the King to march north, fight the Scots in northern England and then join up with Montrose. But there were alternatives. They could march into East Anglia, which had been militarily weakened, or they could aim to fight the New Model before it had been thoroughly trained and blooded. It was because the Committee of Both Kingdoms was conscious of these possibilities that it had ordered Fairfax back from the west to besiege Oxford and told Cromwell to leave Oxford and return to his home at Ely. Cromwell went back expecting to be finally relieved of his commission and to be able to settle down to a private life.

As May was ending Charles still failed to make up his mind whether to move north, east or south. Offered differing pieces of advice, the King was, as usual, vacillating. After recalling Goring from the west, eighteen days later he ordered him to go back there again. In the meantime Charles was persuaded to attack the city of Leicester. The assault was brutal. Some of the defenders were slain in the heat of victory; women and children were found among the dead; the town was given over to plunder. A week later the Royalist army encamped at Daventry (twenty-five miles south of Leicester) where it collected supplies and awaited the arrival of Goring and his cavalry from the west preparatory to marching north again. Although Rupert affected to despise the New Model Army he thought that discretion was the better part of valour and did not thirst for a

'The disposition of a single regiment of infantry in the fields (according to the present discipline of His Majesty King Charles).' The colonel's quarters are in the centre (A–F), near the waggons (Q), and surrounded by the tents and huts of other officers and men; at the bottom are the huts of the sutlers, or suppliers.

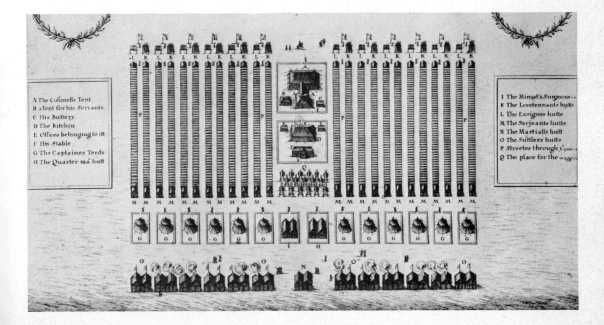

A The Colonells Tent
B a Tent for his Servants
C His Buttery
D The Kitchin
E Offices belonging to it
F His Stable
G The Captaines Tents
H The Quarter ma. hutt

I The Minist & Surgeons
K The Levetennants hutts
L The Ensignes hutts
M The Serjeants hutts
N The Martialls hutt
O The Suttlers hutts
P Streetes through ye
Q The place for the waggon

Henry Ireton (1611–51), Cromwell's trusted friend, who commanded the left wing at Naseby and married Cromwell's daughter Bridget in the following year. At first he favoured conciliation with the King, but in the end, disillusioned, he was one of those who signed Charles's death-warrant in 1649 – the year in which Cooper painted this portrait.

Sir Marmaduke Langdale (1598–1661), whose cavalry were routed by Cromwell at Naseby. He later led a successful campaign in the north, capturing Carlisle and Pontefract Castle in 1648.

battle. The Parliamentarians for their part at last showed military realism. Fairfax was given a free hand. His council of war resolved to seek a decision. Before it did so Fairfax asked Parliament to be allowed to appoint Cromwell as his Lieutenant-General of Horse, although his commission had expired. The Commons consented to his formal reappointment. On 13 June Oliver with six hundred cavalry joined Fairfax at Kislingbury, a village eight miles east of Daventry. By then the King's army had left Daventry where Charles had been relaxing for six days and enjoying a spot of hunting.

The New Model Army was thus within twelve miles of the Royalists before full intelligence of its movements had reached the King. The Royalists then marched from Daventry to Market Harborough, about eighteen miles to the north-east, and encamped there. Charles and Rupert would have liked to get farther away from the New Model Army, especially as Goring had written to say that it was impossible for him to reinforce them immediately. But Fairfax was advancing upon them too fast. Even though the royal troops were awoken at two in the morning of 13 June they had to be assembled from their quarters scattered round Market Harborough. Oliver Cromwell's future son-in-law, Henry Ireton, had caught a group of Royalist soldiers who formed part of the rearguard as they were playing quoits or darts and drinking in the village of Naseby. At midnight a council of war was held in Market Harborough and the King and Prince Rupert concluded that to stand and fight was the best of a number of evils.

The village of Naseby lies seven miles to the south of Market Harborough almost in the very centre of England. It is situated on a plateau about six hundred feet above sea-level; thence flow streams both to the Severn and to the North Sea. The plateau contains low hills and valleys; one of those who fought at Naseby wrote of 'a place of little hills and vales, the ground some ploughed, some champion' (unenclosed). The Royalists deployed on what was called Dust Hill, a mile south of Market Harborough, the Parliamentarians on Mill Hill. The distance between the two hills is one mile; the area between, known as Broadmoor, was to become the battlefield. When Rupert went out to discover the Parliamentarian dispositions he detected a backward or sidewards movement by his enemies which gave him some cause to believe that they were in retreat or might be caught by surprise: in all probability it was a reconnaissance unit returning to report. In actual fact Fairfax had taken immense care over his dispositions, finally moving his line back behind the crest of the hill. The two fronts were about a mile in extent. Some of the ground was swampy or covered with furze bushes that made it treacherous to cavalry. The mounted men on both sides aimed to avoid such pitfalls.

The battle was an odd affair. Both armies were tired when they started to fight in the morning; the contest was all over in three hours. The Royalists are said to have been numerically inferior:

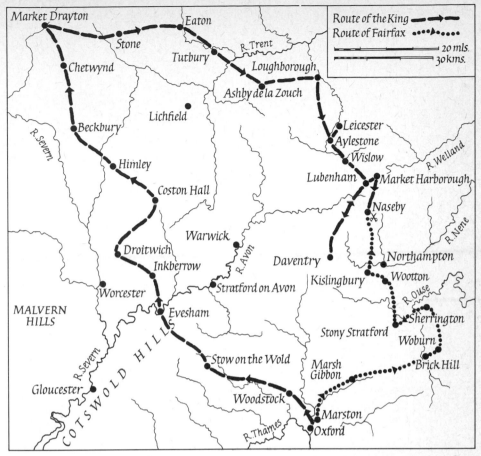

some historians consider that they had 7,500 men, some 9,000 and some over 11,000 against the 13,000 or 14,000 of Fairfax. What is certain is that Rupert had fewer cavalry; he had vainly hoped that Goring's seasoned troopers would have arrived in time to take part in the battle. Furthermore the cavalry who came from Yorkshire led by Sir Marmaduke Langdale were mutinous, being fed up with the war and wanting to go home. The Parliamentarians' morale, on the contrary, was excellent. The cavalry, who had fought for two years under Cromwell, were battle-hardened and religiously inspired. Even the infantry had received some training when they marched into Dorset and back. Finally in spite of low numbers and poor morale Rupert and his brother Maurice began the battle by charging uphill on the right wing.

In a way what happened resembled the events at Marston Moor, except that the troopers hacked at each other with their swords. Though Rupert was now Commander-in-Chief he still could not resist leading the attack. Ireton, who commanded the Parliamentarian left, had attempted to fall on the Royalist infantry; Rupert took advantage of Ireton's distraction and pressed on. Ireton was wounded and overwhelmed. The impetus carried Rupert and his men as far

The campaign culminating in the battle of Naseby, 14 June 1645. After attacking Leicester on 30 May the King's troops moved south to Daventry, then north again, so that on 12–13 June they were encamped around Market Harborough. The Parliamentarian army advanced to meet them from the village of Kislingbury, near Northampton, where Fairfax's troops, who had marched from Oxford, were joined by Cromwell's cavalry.

THE DESCRIPTION OF THE ARMIES OF HO[RSE]

S. Thomas Fairefax his Excellency, as they were drawn

the Fowerteent[h]

Dust Hill

Prince Rupert

Prince Maurice

Sir Bernard Astley

His Forlo[rne]

The King[s Majesty]

The Left Wing Commanded by
Comissa Generall Ireton.

Coll: Butlers Regiment

Coll: Eare

Covington's Regiment
comanded by Sheaffield Regiment

Com-mia Generall I. Ireton

Earle of Man

Earle of Man hope Montgomerie

Maior Generall

Horton Waller

C.L. Riches Regiment

Coll: Fleetwood Regiment

Lieutenant Coll: Pride his
forse

The Mill Hill

The Colls Prid
guard

Mutgrith Hill

Fenny Hill

Larne Leath hill

The traine guarded with forlookes

NASBYE

AND FOOT OF HIS MAJESTIES, AND
…erall bodyes, at the Battayle at NASBYE;
of June 1645

Overleaf: an engraving of the battle of Naseby, 14 June 1645, seen from the Parliamentarian side. To the left of the village is the defended baggage train; above it, the left wing led by Ireton confronts cavalry led by Prince Rupert; in the centre, the King rides alone; on the right, Cromwell faces Sir Marmaduke Langdale. The medallion in the upper right-hand corner shows Sir Thomas Fairfax (*see* p. 83), the parliamentary Commander-in-Chief.

as the enemy baggage-train in Naseby or beyond, just as it had done at Kineton. In the centre in spite of their smaller numbers the Royalist foot managed for a time to hold their own. In view of the number of reluctantly pressed and formerly beaten men to be found in the Parliamentarian ranks that was hardly surprising. On the right, however, Cromwell's cavalry trotting down a steep hill easily broke the Royalist columns. The Lieutenant-General then, as at Marston Moor, rallied his second and third lines of cavalrymen and went to the support of the infantry by attacking the exposed flank of the Royalist centre. The Parliamentarian dragoons, who had been stationed on foot to the extreme left of the battlefield, mounted their nags to attack the Royalist infantry from the other wing. Thus assaulted on both flanks, the Royalist infantrymen recoiled. By the time Rupert returned to the field he could see that all was lost. He joined the King, who with his reserve had been trying to rally the cavalry on the left flank. Together he and his nephew retired to Leicester, fourteen miles away. Some of their cavalry were with them, but their infantry surrendered in droves. Five hundred officers and some 4,500 men were taken prisoners, but only a few hundred were killed in the fighting. All the royal artillery and arms sufficient for 8,000 men were captured. Though the war was to continue for more than another year, the Royalists' cause was ruined and their confidence undermined.

Napoleon was later to stress the value of morale in war. Even more damaging than Charles's defeat at Naseby was the capture of his cabinet containing correspondence with his wife. This disclosed the attempts that he had been making to bring over an Irish army to England and his promise of favours to Roman Catholics. The publication of these letters or drafts of letters showed the peace party on the Parliamentarian side how difficult it would be to reach any agreement with the King, and it equally strengthened the hands of the war party which wished to end the fighting with the complete and utter defeat of the Royalists.

But Charles himself, ever volatile, was not unduly depressed by the battle of Naseby. He was cheered by the continuing successes in Scotland of Montrose who, after his victory at Auldearn, marched south and again outmanoeuvred the Covenanters in a battle at Alford, twenty-five miles west of Aberdeen. The King wrote to Ormonde pressing him to send over troops from Ireland; he thought that he could recruit his infantry in Wales to replace the losses at Naseby; and he even had hopes of French assistance, for the Queen was busily intriguing on his behalf. In the west of England Lord Goring had a small but intact army engaged still on the siege of Taunton. Charles once more hesitated between trying to join Goring in Somerset or Montrose in Scotland. Neither scheme was practical. The Scots had captured Carlisle and in due course the Royalists lost both Pontefract and Scarborough, their two remaining strongholds in Yorkshire. The Scots army began moving south

with the aim of besieging Hereford, Charles's temporary headquarters on the borders of Wales. Meanwhile Fairfax and Cromwell
with the victorious New Model Army were on their way to the
relief of Taunton. The military situation was grasped by Prince
Rupert who recommended the move west as the King's wisest plan,
but was not sanguine about its prospects. In fact Charles went into
Wales to recruit his forces and while he was doing so Goring was
defeated by Fairfax.

The New Model Army, led by Fairfax, had marched rapidly from
Leicester, which surrendered to him after Naseby, and by the
beginning of July had reached Dorset where he pacified the Clubmen – so called because they were armed with clubs – who wanted
to keep both the contending armies out of their part of the world so
as to resume their peaceful occupations. As soon as Goring heard of
the approach of Fairfax he gave up the siege of Taunton, ultimately
drawing up his forces in a strong position covered by the rivers
Yeo and Parrett which join just south of Langport in Somerset.
By feinting at Taunton Goring induced Fairfax to dispatch 4,000
men there, but even then Fairfax's army outnumbered that of the
Royalists. Previously by feinting at Yeovil Fairfax had managed to
persuade Goring to withdraw from his forward positions. Furthermore Goring had sent off most of his artillery to Bridgwater farther
west before he concentrated at Langport. So strategically all was
about square between the two generals.

George, Lord Goring (1608–
57), defeated by Fairfax at
the battle of Langport.
Impatient of discipline and
debauched, he allowed his
troops to ravage the west of
England, making enemies of
the 'Clubmen' who disliked
any fighting over their
counties.

The battle of Langport on 10 July 1645 was a conclusive demonstration of the superior morale of the Parliamentarians. The key to
the battle was a ford across a stream known as the Wagg Rhyne, a
tributary of the Yeo. It was covered on the Royalist side by a ridge
which could be reached solely through a narrow lane with hedges
lining it. Goring posted his only two guns on top of the ridge,
manned the lane with musketeers, and placed his cavalry to the rear.
The Parliamentarian gunners knocked out Goring's cannon; three
troops of cavalry were sent as 'a forlorn hope' to cross the ford and
ride up the lane. This they managed splendidly; though checked by
the Royalist cavalry, they were soon reinforced by a squadron
under Major John Desborough, Oliver Cromwell's brother-in-law.
After a fierce contest the Royalists broke and fled.

Surveying the situation after the battle of Langport, Prince
Rupert advised the King to conclude peace. Charles replied:

> If I had any other quarrel but the defence of my religion, crown and
> friends, you had full reason for your advice; for I confess that, speaking
> as a mere soldier or statesman, I must say there is no probability but
> my ruin; yet, as a Christian, I must tell you that God will not suffer
> rebels and traitors to prosper, nor this cause to be overthrown . . .

That was Charles at his noblest, while the letter helps to show how
completely both sides believed that the Lord of Hosts would fight
for them. And indeed a ray of hope lit the Royalist shadows as

autumn approached. Taking advantage of Cromwell's absence in the west, the King daringly raided Huntingdon, Cromwell's birth-place, which was given over to plunder. While he was there he learned that the heroic Montrose had crossed the Firth of Forth near Stirling to inflict yet another defeat on the Covenanters at Kilsyth, only ten miles north-west of Glasgow. Argyll, who was with the Covenanters, fled for safety to Berwick on Tweed, while other fugitives rode as far as Carlisle. Montrose appeared to be the master of Scotland. The Scottish army in England had no alternative but to abandon the siege of Hereford and dispatch the bulk of their cavalry home. King Charles, who returned safely to Oxford after the raid on Huntingdon, was able to sally forth to Hereford, optimistically aiming to raise another army. But soon his hopes of recovery were ruined. On 11 September Prince Rupert surrendered Bristol, the most valuable town in the possession of the Royalists, to General Fairfax. Rupert did not have a big enough garrison to protect the five-mile circumvallation of the city, while the morale of both soldiers and civilians was at its lowest ebb. The King at once dismissed Rupert from all his offices, condemning him for a 'mean action' which tried both his faith and his belief in his nephew's loyalty. But Rupert was merely accepting the military facts. Two days later Montrose was at last defeated by the reinforced Covenanters at the battle of Philiphaugh near Selkirk in the Lowlands. Those of his followers who were not killed in the battle were executed as traitors by the orders of Argyll and the Presbyterian ministers of God on the Scottish council of war. Montrose himself managed to escape to the Highlands. After Langport and Philiphaugh the first civil war was virtually over.

The King hardly knew which way to turn. Leaving the west, he tried vainly to go north, but eventually rode east to arrive in Newark. Here undignified squabbling between Charles's advisers and courtiers broke out. Rupert arrived there on 16 October determined that the besmirchment of his name should be removed. Under pressure Charles concurred with the findings of a council of war that his nephew had been guilty of neither cowardice nor disloyalty, but he refused to employ the Prince any more in his service.

The King left Newark to return to Oxford at the beginning of November. Here he was to learn of the comprehensive mopping-up operations of the New Model Army in Wiltshire, Cornwall, Devon, Dorset and Hampshire. Cromwell laid siege to Basing House in Hampshire, long known as 'Loyalty House'. It was symbolic of the changed fortunes of war that two distinguished artists formerly in the employment of the King, Wenceslaus Hollar, the engraver, and Inigo Jones, the architect, were both found there by the Parliamentarians having been engaged in planning its defences. Jones, whose responsibility for arranging the Queen's lovely masques in Whitehall Palace was not appreciated by the Puritans, was stripped naked and carried away in a blanket. Two other enduring strong-

Opposite: Basing House, the mansion of the Roman Catholic Marquis of Winchester, commanded the road to the west through Salisbury and had been repeatedly besieged by Parliamentarians before Cromwell overwhelmed it in October 1645. An engraving, *above*, shows the old and new parts of the house (A and B), the 'tower that is half battered doune' (C), the King's breastworks (D) and the Parliamentarian breastworks (E). During the sacking by Cromwell's troops the house caught fire, and its fortifications were later razed: little now remains but overgrown mounds and the foundations of the buildings (*below*). Of the defenders some 100 were slaughtered; among the prisoners were the artists Hollar (1607–77), *centre left*, and Inigo Jones (1573–1652), *centre right* (drawn by Van Dyck).

holds of royalism, Hereford and Chester, also surrendered that autumn; the loss of Chester meant that all hope of succour from Ireland had to be given up by the King. Henceforward he devoted himself to elaborate diplomatic manœuvres.

In spite of all his ingenuities the King knew in his heart of hearts that his cause was in peril. Twice he ordered his eldest son to leave England for France. Reluctantly the young Prince obeyed, eventually reaching his mother in Paris by way of the Scilly Isles and Channel Islands. His former military adviser, Lord Hopton, lingered in Cornwall for some days only to watch his remaining soldiers deserting to the other side so that he himself had to surrender honourably to Fairfax.

After the new campaigning season began in the spring of 1646 Charles escaped from Oxford in disguise and slowly found his way to the headquarters of the Scottish army, which was encamped at Southwell between Nottingham and Newark. The day after he arrived Newark surrendered to the Scots, while five days later Fairfax summoned Oxford. Articles of capitulation were finally signed on 24 June. The King's second son, the Duke of York (the future James II) thus became a prisoner of Parliament, which already

Chester, the port through which troops and supplies were brought from Ireland; on the left is the medieval castle, with the town beyond it, on the right the Dee bridge. The town's surrender to Parliament ended the King's hope of rescue from Ireland.

held two of his sisters. The King himself was taken by the Scots to Newcastle upon Tyne where he refused either to promise the Scots to accept Presbyterianism as the dominant religion in England or to agree to nineteen humiliating propositions sent to him from London. Instead he played golf and chess, engaged in theological arguments and procrastinated. Eventually the victorious English Parliamentarians decided to pay off the Scottish army, furnishing the first instalment of the money in January 1647. The King himself was handed over to English Commissioners who conducted him to honourable captivity at Holmby House in Northamptonshire.

Can it be said that the first civil war had any important social or economic consequences? London certainly had become more puritanical. With the departure of the Court the theatres were closed. No longer were there masques and dancing. The King's splendid collection of paintings was to be sold and dispersed. Long sermons were addressed to Parliament in all times of victory or crisis. Fast-days were frequent. London became a dismal town, especially during the early war years suffering shortages of food and fuel, while wounded men, war widows and orphans swelled the ranks of the city beggars. In Oxford, on the other hand, although

Newark was besieged by a
combined force of English
and Scottish troops from
6 March to 8 May 1646. The
defences included the town's
own fortifications and
outworks such as the Queen's
Sconce, immediately to the
north-west of the town
(visible on the plan, *right*),
which, though it failed to
prevent Newark's surrender,
still survives today (*above*).

it was a military headquarters, with New College turned into a magazine and cattle herded into Christ Church quadrangle, every effort was made in an overcrowded city to maintain the pomp and magnificence of the royal Court. The King appointed a Master of Revels and brought the painter William Dobson there so that he might portray members of the royal family and royal heroes such as Prince Rupert. But duels and drunken brawls were commonplace, while the King's advisers busily intrigued against one another. Outside London and Oxford life went on much as before except in those areas where fighting was taking place. Though yeomen and smallholders are often said to have all sided with Parliament, in fact the Clubmen, (who would have preferred to be neutral and vainly tried to keep the war outside the boundaries of their own particular counties) were chiefly yeomen. Some great castles such as Corfe in Dorset and Basing House in Hampshire were destroyed or left empty shells.

But the character of local government changed little. Justices of the Peace continued to function as before, while the county committees preserved law and order. Even after the Royalists had been defeated there, the administration in Cornwall was carried out by exactly the same gentry class as had ruled before the war. In Suffolk, which was never Royalist, the county committee was 'a kind of exclusive club comprising much of the brains and much of the wealth of the shire'. Admittedly Royalist gentry had their lands sequestrated until fines levied upon them were paid in full. But often they quietly transferred their properties to friends who had fought on the opposite side. In the long run, modern research suggests, no significant change in the distribution of landed property took place as a result of the war.

In London wounded men, war widows and orphans swelled the ranks of city beggars. When the war ended in 1647 the rank and file of the army asked for pensions for dependants of men killed in the fighting, but they met a violent opposition in Parliament and no payments were made.

Royalist Oxford. *Right:* the city fortified in
1644 (the view has been reversed, as it was
drawn back to front: *see note* p. 186).
Below: a crown minted at Oxford, showing
the King and the city. *Bottom:* William
Dobson (1610–46), painter to the
Court in exile.

What of the common people? They suffered most in parts of the country which were overrun by soldiers requiring food, horses and 'free quarter', which was not at once paid for. On the other hand, the demands of war created full employment and increased the earnings of labour. Some ordinary men were glad to enlist in an army or navy to secure a share of plunder. The principal grievance was the new taxes, particularly the excise which was imposed, among other things, upon ale, the chief solace of the poor. Veronica Wedgwood has observed that

> young men who had never seen anything but, at best, the parlour of some small squire's houses, now entered as conquerors some of the greatest houses in England, stared with wonder, or envy, or austere

Opposite: the Royalist stronghold of Corfe Castle in Dorset, dismantled by the Parliamentarians after its capture in 1646.

A contemporary caricature of a pillaging soldier. In place of a musket he holds a goose on a spit; his shield is a dripping-pan; bottles of wine hang from his cross-belt; he is gartered with black pots; his sword is replaced by an artichoke; and on his head instead of a feathered hat he wears a tripod pot, decorated with a duck. (For an idea of the costume parodied, *see* p. 75.)

Bolsover Castle in Derbyshire, the magnificent house of the Marquis of Newcastle. He left England for the Continent after the Royalist defeat at Marston Moor in 1644, and Bolsover was later taken by the Parliamentarians. This illustration, showing the Marquis himself on horseback in front of the castle, is taken from a book on horsemanship which he published abroad in 1658.

disapproval at the stately splendours of Welbeck, or Bolsover or Raglan Castle, or Lathom House . . . [yet] there is relatively little trace of vindictiveness of the poor against the rich in anything they said or did.

But freed from the authority of the Church and Royalist officials radical ideas developed and old shibboleths were questioned.

Two social consequences of the civil war may be stressed: the first is that the atmosphere of Royalist Oxford became a pattern for the dissolute and backbiting Court of Charles II where standards of sexual morality were low and of corruption high. The second is that the freedom of thought engendered both in the Parliamentarian army and among the radical sects meant that the monopolistic authority of the Church of England was permanently undermined. In the economic life of the kingdom after the Restoration the most significant influence was upon the growth of overseas trade. The impression of power spread abroad by the renown of the New Model Army and the Commonwealth navy paved the way for the conclusion of valuable treaties which were to pay dividends for the British Commonwealth.

Chapter Seven

THE SECOND CIVIL WAR 1648

Once the first civil war was won the effective rulers of England, who were concentrated in the House of Commons and the reduced House of Lords, had two problems before them: how to demobilize or get rid of their armies and how to come to a settlement with the defeated King. Before Charles left Newcastle he had been presented with modified proposals to which it was hoped that he might consent: by these Parliament would control the armed forces for ten years and Presbyterianism was to become the national religion for three years, though the King himself was not required to accept the Covenant. Had Charles agreed to these proposals he might at once have been restored to his throne. But, as usual, he played for time, hoping, like Mr Micawber, that something would turn up.

The handling of the New Model Army by the parliamentary leaders was much clumsier. For it was determined that half the army should be disbanded, that the remainder should be sent to Ireland or employed on mobile policing duties in England, and that apart from the Commander-in-Chief no officers above the rank of colonel should be retained in service. Furthermore no member of parliament was to continue as an officer in the army and no clear provision was made about the payment of arrears or an amnesty for offences. If the peace party in Parliament had their way, they could put the army under the orders of officers they trusted and by thus wielding the power of the sword ensure that the King was loyal to the constitutional settlement which they wanted.

The New Model Army, which for the past two years had been marching about England destroying property and living on 'free quarter', was naturally unpopular with civilians. Petitions were dispatched to Parliament asking for its prompt disbandment. But the army was unwilling to agree to demobilization except on fair conditions. Thus antagonism arose between a majority of the Parliament and the victorious soldiers.

During the spring of 1647 three parliamentary deputations were sent to meet the army officers at Saffron Walden, then the military

Christ Church Coll: Ox: Canterbury Minster   Trinn: Colledge Camb:

MERCURIUS
RUSTICUS
1685.

Countess of Rivers plundered pag: 11

S.ʳ John Lucas house plundered pag: 1.

S.ʳ Rich: Mynshul hous plundered pag: 31.

THE
COUNTRYS
COMPLAINT
Recounting
the sad
Events
of the late
unparalleld
REBELLION

A Bonfire for the voting downe Episcopacy pag: 26.

M.ʳ Jones a Mini: carried on a Beare pag: 81.

Edge hill   Battle

Warder Castle defended by a Lady. pag: 41.

1685.

The Souldiers in their passage to York turn unto reformers pull down Popish pictures, break down rayles, turn altars into Tables.

headquarters. The first deputation was told bluntly that more information was needed about the conditions of demobilization and the arrangements for the expedition to Ireland. That was hardly an unreasonable demand on the part of the officers; the rank-and-file at the same time drew up a petition to Fairfax seeking arrears and indemnities and asking that pensions should be paid to widows and orphans of men killed in the war. Over this petition the parliamentary leaders took umbrage and in a thin House of Commons voted in favour of a declaration that those soldiers who 'in their distempered condition . . . go on advancing and promoting that petition shall be looked upon and proceeded against as enemies of the State and disturbers of the public peace'.

Such was the atmosphere of mutual distrust when the second deputation reached Saffron Walden. No concessions were offered by either side. Fairfax was instructed to order his men to volunteer for service in Ireland under Philip Skippon, a commander highly trusted in London, while the officers were told they should urge their men to volunteer. Fairfax retorted that he would express his wishes, which were usually granted, but would not issue commands; he then retired to bed with influenza at his mother-in-law's house. The officers insisted that they would do nothing until arrears had been met and an indemnity given.

At last the parliamentary leaders began to see sense. They voted that six weeks' arrears should be paid at once and they dispatched

Parliamentarian soldiers in Yorkshire undoing Laud's work – destroying 'Popish' paintings and altar furniture, and smashing the communion rails which separated the congregation from the altar.

Opposite: 'the sad Events of the late unparalleld rebellion', as recalled in 1685, include the fortification of Oxford and Cambridge, the plundering of three great houses and the humiliation of ministers of religion (one is forced to ride on a bear).

FIVE ORDERS
AND ORDINANCE
Of Parliament, For payment of Souldiers.
VIZ.

1 For such Souldiers as conforme to the Votes of both Houses sent downe to the Army, shall receive the benefit of those Votes. 2. For one Moneths pay to certaine Officers in the Foure Lists. 3. For one moneths pay to certaine Officers whose Accompts are not Stated. 4. For six weekes pay to those Officers whose Accompts are Stated. 5. For appointing of severall persons Treasurers for receiving and paying of monies to the Souldiers, at Weavers-Hall in London.

Die Veneris 11 Iunii 1647.

ORdered by the Lords and Commons in Parliament assembled, That all such Officers or Souldiers of the Army, as shall come off and conform to the Votes sent down to the Army, shall receive the benefit and advantage of those Votes.   *Hen. Elsynge Cler. Parl. Dom. Com.*

Iunii 15. 1647

ORdered by the Lords and Commons assembled in Parliament, That the Treasurers at *Christ-Church* do pay upon Saturday next, unto the officers nominated in the foure lists or to their Executors or assignes, reported to this house about *November* last past, one moneths pay according to the establishment of the Army under the Command of Sir *Thomas Fairfax* for their present relief, untill such summes of money otherwise ordered towards their satisfaction may be received.   *Hen. Elsynge Cler. Parl. Dom. Com.*

15 Junii 1647,

ORdered by the Lords and Commons assembled in Parliament that the Treasurers at *Christ-Church* do upon the sixteenth of this instant *June* pay unto those officers in Commission that are now attending in this town whose accompts are not yet stated (upon producing sufficient certificates under the hands of their respective Commanders in chief, which shall containe the time of their actuall service for the Parliament and qualities) one moneths pay of their arrears according to the establishment of the Army, under the command of Sir *Thomas Fairfax* and upon the determination of their accounts according to the ordinance and instructions of the 28 of *May* last, 2 moneths pay more with the same security for the remainder as is voted and ordered to the officers of the said Army, provided that this extend not to the Officers of the trained Bands or Auxiliary Regiments of this City, or to the other officers for whom other provisions hath been lately made by any order of both, or either of the Houses of Parliament, or to any other Officer whose name is not already listed, or shall not be listed before the said sixteenth of this instant in the list lately brought into this House by Collonell *Sands*, Collonell *Devoreux*, and others, and to be by them compleated.   *Hen. Elsynge Cler. Parl. Dom. Com.*

June the 15. 1647.

ORdered by the Lords and Commons assembled in Parliament that the Treasurers at Christchurch do upon Thursday next pay unto the Officers in Commission (who have attended in this Towne and have their accompts stated by the authority of Parliament though not according to the instructions lately published, and have received no money thereupon) six weeks pay, according to the establishment of the Army, under the command of Sir *Thomas Fairfax*, and indorse the summe so paid upon every such account, provided that this extend not to the Officers who are already otherwise provided for, by order of both, or either Houses of Parliament. And it is further ordered and declared that such officers whose accounts are stated by authority of Parliament, and not already satisfied, and shall not be willing to stay to have them determined according to the instructions aforesaid, may hereafter present Lists of such acounts by the Committee of the Military Garden to this house to the intent they may receive the same proportion and securities given to others upon such accompts.   *Hen. Elsynge Cler. Parl. D. Com.*

Whereas, by a former Ordinance bearing date the sixteenth of this instant June, 1647. it is ordained, that the summe of 22000 l. to make the 5000 l. formerly charged upon *Weavers Hall* 27000 l. be paid by Alderman *Bunch* and the rest of the Treasurers at *Weavers Hall* and to Mr. *Pococke*, Mr. *Greenhill*, and the rest of the Treasurers at Christ-Church to be issued as by the said Ordinance is appointed.

And whereas divers of the Treasurers aforesaid are not in Towne which hinders the execution of the service : It is therefore ordained by the Lords and Commons, that Mr. *Blackwell* and Mr. *Ashurst* Citizens of *London*, shall be and are hereby added to be Treasurers for the receiving and issuing the money aforesaid together with Mr. *Greenhill* and Mr. *Pococke*, and that the acquittances of them, or any two of them shall be sufficient discharge unto the said Alderman *Bunch*, and the rest of the Treasurers, at Weavers Hall.

And it is further Ordained, that the said Treasurers shall have the allowance of one penny in the pound for performance of the said service, and for satisfying of the Officers, and such as they shall appoint under them in such manner as they shall thinke fit.

And whereas by another Ordinance of the same date, divers Field-Officers and Auditors are nominated and appointed to renew and examine the severall Accompts and Certificates of the Officers which are to receive any money from the said Treasurers.

It is further Ordered and Ordained that any three Field-Officers with any one of the Auditor nominated in the Ordinance aforesaid, signing such Certificates, Tickets, or accompts, it shall be a sufficient Warrant and discharge unto the said Mr. *Pocock* and the rest of the Treasurers by this and the former Ordinance appointed, for the issuing out and paying the money aforesaid unto the Officers, according unto the severall Ordinances already passed in that behalf.

And whereas Mr. *Pocock*, Mr. *Greenhill* and others, have formerly been appointed Treasurers by an Ordinance of the date aforesaid, for the receiving and issuing out of ten thousand pounds to the private Souldiery. Forasmuch, and in regard of other employments, they cannot conveniently attend that service. It is therefore ordained, that Collonel *Gower Anthony Bickerstaffe* Mr. *Iames Story*, Mr. *Maximilian* Beard, Citizens of *London*, shall bee, and are hereby nominated and appointed Treasurers for the receiving, issuing and paying the ten thousand pounds aforesaid. And that they or any two of their acquittances shall be a sufficient discharge unto Mr. Alderman *Bunch*, and the rest of the Treasurers at Weavers Hall.

And it is further Ordained, that the said Collonel *Gower* and the rest of the Treasurers hereby appointed, shall bee allowed one penny in the pound for themselves, and their Officers employed in this service in such manner as they shall think fit.

ORdered by the Commons assembled in Parliament, that these Orders and Ordinance be forthwith Printed and published.   *Hen. Elsynge, Cler. Parl. Dom. Com.*

LONDON,
Printed for *Edward Husband*, Printer to the Honourable House of Commons, 1647.

A group of medieval and Tudor houses in Saffron Walden including the Sun Inn, far right, where in the spring of 1647 commissioners from Parliament, and later Cromwell, Ireton, Fleetwood and Skippon, are thought to have met representatives of the New Model Army in an attempt to heal the division in the Parliamentarian side.

four army officers who were also members of parliament, including Cromwell, Ireton and Skippon, to treat with the army at Saffron Walden and quench its fears. They returned with the report that, provided satisfactory arrangements were made about their arrears, the soldiers would disband peaceably but would not hear of going to Ireland. Earlier the Speaker had been told that the army was unsettled and suffering from a deep sense of its grievances; indeed the soldiers promptly observed that they were to be given only six or eight weeks' pay when more than a year's pay was owing to them. Fairfax was told that his men wanted a general meeting of the whole of the army in which each regiment should have its own representatives – known as 'adjutants' or 'agitators' – to put their point of view. Fairfax gave way and on 4 June the whole of the army camped near Newmarket. Here Cromwell as well as Fairfax joined it.

The growing hostility between Parliament and the army warmed the heart of the royal captive. Charles assured the Speaker of the House of Lords that he accepted in principle the latest proposals submitted to him, but he asked permission to come to Westminster so that he might as king give his assent to the Bills necessary to

Opposite: a parliamentary proclamation published in June 1647 setting forth categories of officers to be paid, and the means of collecting and distributing the necessary money. No mention is made of payment to ordinary soldiers. Such orders did little to dispel the army's sense of grievance towards Parliament.

THE

Declaration and Standard

Of the *Levellers* of *England*;
Delivered in a Speech to his Excellency the Lord Gen. *Fairfax*,
on *Friday* last at White-Hall, by Mr. *Everard*, a late Member of the
Army, and his Prophesie in reference thereunto; shewing what will
befall the Nobility and Gentry of this Nation, by their submitting to
community; With their invitation and promise unto the people, and
their proceedings in *Windsor* Park, *Oatlands* Park, and severall other
places; also, the Examination and confession of the said Mr. *Everard*
before his Excellency, the manner of his deportment with his Hat on,
and his severall speeches and expressions, when he was commanded
to put it off. Together with a List of the severall Regiments of Horse
and Foot that have cast Lots to go for *Ireland*.

Imprinted at *London*, for *G. Laurinson*, *Aprill 23. 1649.*

'They have given themselves a new name; viz., Levellers, for they intend to sett all things straight, and rayse a parity and community in the kingdom.' The Levellers, who were influential in the army, were opposed to Charles I's autocracy and critical of Parliament. The pamphlet was their weapon: this one is typical of the many published from 1647 onwards.

implement the agreement. Evidently he hoped now that Parliament and the army were quarrelling to be accepted as an instrument or symbol of national conciliation. But if that was his idea, it was frustrated by a *coup* organized by the army agitators. A very junior officer, Cornet Joyce, collected a force of five hundred men, marched to Holmby House, and seized the King. When Joyce was asked by Charles for his warrant, he significantly pointed to the soldiers under his orders.

From the beginning of June when the King was taken into the hands of the army and when the army itself disobeyed orders to

142

disband, the whole character of public affairs changed. Hitherto the spokesmen for the army had been content with putting forward their own specific grievances. But the attitude of Parliament chilled the soldiers' loyalty. Concessions granted to Parliament by former soldiers already disbanded (known as 'Reformadoes') and to the fathers of the City of London, who commanded a trained militia, aroused fears that a new internecine war was imminent. The New Model Army had no wish to fight Parliament but it sought a constitutional settlement which would embrace the soldiers' own claims for decent treatment now the war was over. Thus when after the seizure of the King the army leaders started drawing up declarations it moved forward towards framing political proposals. These proposals may well be linked with the evolution of the Leveller movement, led by John Lilburne, himself a former Lieutenant-Colonel, whose 'large petition' published in March 1647 had social and economic overtones. Cromwell and other principal army officers might still aver that the settlement of the kingdom should be left to Parliament and that 'when the State has once made a settlement we [soldiers] have nothing to say but submit and suffer', but they were being gradually driven to taking up a more positive attitude: a 'Declaration of the Army' dated 15 June, drawn up by the Council of the Army, which included representatives of the rank-and-file as well as officers, claimed the army's right to speak in the name of the English people since it was not 'a mere mercenary

John Lilburne (c. 1614–57), the leader of the Levellers, standing at the bar during his trial in the London Guildhall in 1649, when he was accused of sedition. The portrait is taken from a broadsheet published to celebrate his acquittal.

army hired to serve any arbitrary power of a State, but called forth and conjured by several declarations of Parliament to the defence of their own and the people's just rights and liberties'. Parliament was therefore required to purge itself of obnoxious members and to fix a date for its own dissolution.

It is not possible to describe in detail the political and constitutional arguments of the different sides which were reproduced in pamphlets and broadsheets during the rest of 1647. But first should be considered the position of the King whose actions brought about the second war. While he was a prisoner of the army he went on negotiating, auctioneering, as it were, the value of his services to the community. At one time he rejected the draft proposals put forward by the army in a document drawn up by Henry Ireton known as *The Heads of the Proposals*. Later Charles accepted this as a basis for discussion and it was indeed modified in an attempt to satisfy him. At the same time a number of prominent Scotsmen including the first Duke of Hamilton and the Earl of Lauderdale were offering to help Charles back to authority provided he met their religious demands. To Cromwell and Ireton the King promised toleration of religious dissenters; to the Scots, on the contrary, he spoke of suppressing the sects. While the Council of the Army was considering fresh political schemes Charles escaped from imprisonment in Hampton Court, where he had been moved by the army, and fled to the Isle of Wight. Evidently he imagined that he would obtain a freer hand in negotiating there and that if the worst came to the worst he could find a ship and leave for France. But his attempts to escape were to prove abortive. Finally he consented to the Scots' religious requirements. He agreed to the establishment of a Presbyterian system for three years, to allow an assembly of divines to draw up a permanent settlement of the Church, and to put down the Independents and other sects. In return the Scots engaged to restore him safe and free to his throne.

Before that engagement was reached the English military commanders had decided to coerce Parliament. On 6 August the army entered London and eleven of the leaders in the Commons who had been most critical of the soldiers fled. The army then withdrew to Putney, a few miles from Westminster, to reconsider the whole political situation. Under Leveller influence a republican movement was beginning to emerge, though this was not specifically stated. Cromwell, who took the chair at army debates held in Putney, was willing to come to terms with the King if that was the only effective means of restoring peace and order to the country. On 20 October 1647 he delivered a three-hour speech in the Commons opposing a motion that no further negotiations should take place unless Charles accepted the rigorous terms put to him at Newcastle and elsewhere. However once it became known at the end of the year that Charles, after fleeing to the Isle of Wight, had come to a secret agreement with the Scots Commissioners, Parliamentarians and army officers closed their ranks. A vote was carried in the Commons to stop negotiations with the King and orders were given that he should be subjected to closer surveillance.

What were the immediate causes of the second civil war? Undoubtedly the failure of the English political nation to conclude a settlement with the King was the main factor. Though the republican movement had been strengthened by the course of events and there was talk of impeaching and deposing Charles I, more people adhered to the view that the monarchy must remain the headstone of satisfactory government. Secondly, two sources of resentment prevailed. The first was growing dissatisfaction with the imposition of Puritanism in its most disagreeable and censorious forms. The second was the unpopularity of many county committees which had been set up during the first civil war to raise money and recruit soldiers, afterwards being given powers to sequester and administer Royalist estates.

As local historians have pointed out, the county committee 'had no clearly defined authority over the civil population', but 'civil and military affairs were so closely entangled that it could not avoid taking upon itself the solution of many overtly civil problems.' Moreover since usually the Clerk of the Peace and Justices of the Peace in sympathy with Parliament were members of the committee, in effect they came to rule as a kind of local oligarchy. Sometimes a virtual dictatorship emerged. In Kent Sir Anthony Welden, an elderly, bitter and disappointed man, was the local boss and so was a Puritan extremist, Sir John Pyne, in Somerset. Thus a rising which took place in Kent in the spring of 1648 was not so much positively Royalist as an active protest against 'the thing called a committee'. That was why it was supported by 'nearly all the indigenous Kentish families who had formed the backbone of the moderate party since 1640'. But it was because the intensity of grievances against the Parliamentarian régime varied from county to county that the Royalists proved incapable of co-ordinating revolts in the second civil war. The numerous rebels in Kent failed to come to an agreement with the Royalists in neighbouring Essex; the consequence was that the Kentish rising was put down by General Fairfax almost before the men of Essex took up their arms. Similarly the discontented citizens in London were not approached by George Goring, Earl of Norwich, who had been sent to take control in south-east England, until the necessary military precautions to suppress an outbreak had been completed. Though half the navy declared itself for the King in July, Charles, Prince of Wales, who took command of the revolted warships, failed to succour the risings in Kent or Essex. Finally Royalist defenders of the city of Colchester, who gallantly held out against Fairfax for ten weeks, were already at their last gasp by the time the news of the defeat of the Scottish 'Engagers' in Lancashire reached them. Thus whereas the Royalists in the first civil war survived so long against the superior resources and arms of

The King escaped from Hampton Court and fled to the Isle of Wight in November 1647 hoping to obtain greater freedom of action; when he left it in December 1648 after a year's imprisonment in Carisbrooke Castle, it was to stand trial.

Right: Charles with Colonel Robert Hammond, Governor of the Isle of Wight, who was torn in his loyalty and finally dismissed by the army. (The pamphlet also refers to the pro-Royalist revolt of the navy and the mutiny in Wales of Colonel Poyer, commander of Pembroke Castle.)

A Royalist print (*opposite above*) shows the King in Carisbrooke Castle, from which he repeatedly planned escapes, smuggling letters out via his chambermaid, Mary. The note shown here (*opposite below*) was written on 31 January 1648 – 1647 by the old calendar – when the King had been a prisoner for exactly a month.

HIS
Maiesties Demands to
Collonel HAMMOND,

Delivered in the Presence-Chamber, upon the discovery of another great Designe, for the conveying of His Majesties person from *Carisbrook* Castle. With Collonel *Hammonds* Answer thereunto.

Alfo, the Oath of Secrefie taken by the Seamen of the revolted Ships, concerning the King, and the difperfing of them and their pretended Vice-Admirall, on the Irifh Seas.

Together, with the taking of *Tinby* Caftle in Southwales, by Collonel *Horton*; with all the Ordnance, Armes and Ammunition; and the further proceedings of Collonel *Poyer* at Pembrook Caftle thereupon.

LONDON. Printed by *I. C.* for *R. W.* 1648.

Parliament because they enjoyed central direction from the King, in the second civil war Parliamentarian armies were skilfully marshalled by Fairfax while the Royalist military effort lacked unity, for the King was a closely guarded prisoner and Prince Rupert, who had returned to Holland, was no longer able to guide strategy or to infuse his energy into the war.

The scattered risings which reflected a reaction in favour of the King had begun when on 9 April the Lord Mayor of London sent a party of militia to prevent a crowd of boys from playing tip-cat in Moorfields on the Sabbath day. A crowd of apprentices took the

Behold your King

THE
ILE
OF WAIT

Monday 31: Jan: 1647.

Mary send this inclosed, to him, from whom you receaued
that, wch I found yesterday under the Carpet: but there is
a seruice of more importance, wch I hope you may doe me, that
now, it being late, I cannot ▓▓▓ particularly tell you of: I could
best doe it by word of mouth, but for too much notice; wch I leaue
to your judgement, wherfore if I fynde you not in my Bed=
chamber the morrow after dinner, I will wryte it so you,
as well as I can: C R

A Harmany of Healths,

To the Kings happy Vnion,
With the Parliaments Commuňion,
To the Princes comming heither,
To the two Dukes together,
To th'two *Maryes* prosperity,
And the rest o'th' Posterity.

The Tune is,   *Give the Word about, &c.*

COme honest Neighbours all,
  sith we are met here,
For the best Wine let's call,
  that we can get here:
Let's in a merry vaine
  all cares abandon,
King Charles will come againe,
  shortly to London.
Her's to our Royall King,
  in *Spanish* Fountaines,
And to the blest off-spring,
  Prince of the *Mountaines:*
I neither dread rebukes,
  nor aduersaries,
Here's a Health to both the Dukes,
  and the two *Maries.*

They who are Subjects true,
  faithfull and loyall,
Will yeild obedience due,
  t'our Soveraigne Loyall:
The King of Heaven did
  o're us instate him,
I would the Land were rid
  of all that hate him.
Here's to our Royall King, &c.

With sad and heavy cheare,
  we all have smarted, (deare,
Since Charles our Soveraigne
  from us departed:
And since his Consort mild,
  sayl'd to her Brother,
And Charles their princely Child,
  went to his Mother.
Heres a bealth to our royall king &c

I wish with all my Soule,
  that the first Movers,
Of this Distraction foule,
  those mischiefe Lovers:
May have their due deserts,
  play all good Fellowes,
That they in severall Carts,
  may ride to'th' Gallowes.
Here's a Health to our royall King.
  in *Spanish* Fountaines,
And to the blest off-spring,
  Prince of the *Mountaines*
I neither dread rebukes,
  nor aduersaries,
Here's a Health to both our Dukes,
  and the two *Maries.*

side of the boys and marched along Fleet Street and the Strand towards Whitehall. Cromwell ordered his cavalry to charge the mob which was forced to break up. But the episode was a warning of the temper of ordinary people in the City. A not dissimilar riot had taken place in Canterbury at Christmas 1647 when the Mayor had forbidden the usual festivities and tried to compel the shops to stay open. His orders were defied, holly bushes placed at street doors, and cries were heard of the need to release the King. Though, as in London, the military suppressed the riot after ten days the discontent of even moderate men presaged the rebellion in Kent in the early spring. Such were the sort of demonstrations in England. In South Wales during April the Colonel in command of Pembroke Castle aroused the county and declared for the King and the Book of Common Prayer. By May it was learnt in London that the Engagers in Scotland were mobilizing an army and by the end of the month an attempt by King Charles to escape from the Isle of Wight was known to have taken place and to have failed. In the middle of the month there were stirrings in Surrey as well as Kent but by 1 June Fairfax had occupied the county capital of Maidstone and the Kentish field force of some 8,000 volunteers headed by men recently released from prison was dispersed, only 500 getting away to Rochester, eventually to join the Essex Royalists under the command of the Earl of Norwich.

Pembroke Castle, whose commander, Colonel Poyer, declared for the King and was defeated by Cromwell in the second civil war.

Opposite: a song-sheet printed in London, hoping for the King's return to the city, and wishing death to 'the first Movers of this Distraction foule'.

Major-General John Lambert (1619–84), commander of the Parliamentarian forces in the north until Cromwell's arrival during the second civil war. In the summer of 1647 he had worked with Ireton to draw up *The Heads of the Proposals*, presenting the army's case to the King.

At this very time a Royalist force in the north of England had gathered under the command of Sir Marmaduke Langdale, who after occupying Carlisle organized the capture of Pontefract Castle by a stratagem. Later Royalists occupied Scarborough Castle. Major-General John Lambert, who had been the Parliamentarian commander in the north since the previous summer, was obliged to send a detachment to besiege Pontefract Castle, while he himself watched Langdale's movements in Cumberland. Thus for a while the Royalists held Rochester, Dover, Deal, Chelmsford, Pembroke, Pontefract, Scarborough and Carlisle while unrest showed itself in the City of London and permeated the fleet stationed in the Downs.

The most remarkable victory of the second civil war was the battle-and-rout of Preston, and the most dramatic episode was the defence of Colchester by the Royalists. Cromwell, after some difficulties owing to the temporary loss of his siege-guns in the mud of the Severn, defeated the rebel Colonel and occupied Pembroke Castle on 11 July. Three days earlier the Duke of Hamilton and the Scottish Engagers had entered England and begun to march south via Carlisle and Preston aiming for Manchester and North Wales. Fairfax ordered Cromwell to join Lambert in the north. By mid

August Oliver, pausing only to reinforce the troops besieging Pontefract, marched his army at the rate of ten miles a day and linked up with Lambert at Otley near Leeds in Yorkshire. Neither side really knew what the other was doing. Hamilton finally decided not to go into Yorkshire but to continue his march through Lancashire. Besides his army of some 9,000 to 10,000 Scots, Langdale commanded 3,000 or 4,000 English Royalists while Sir George Monro managed to bring 2,100 foot and 1,200 horse across the Irish sea to fight for the King. As Hamilton was reinforced by another 4,000 raised in Scotland within a month of his own departure, the Scots and Royalists in the north amounted to over 20,000 men. The Parliamentarian army under Cromwell and Lambert consisted of only about 9,000, but they were more experienced and with a higher morale than their enemy. The Scots were inadequately armed and provisioned, they were encumbered by women camp-followers and the weather was unpleasant in the extreme. Cromwell was informed incorrectly that Hamilton was waiting at Preston for the arrival of Monro's men. On 16 August after holding a council of war in the Pennines, which divide Yorkshire from Lancashire, Cromwell resolved to advance along the north bank of the River Ribble so as to cut off Hamilton from his base in Scotland.

As it happened, by the time the Parliamentarians reached Preston Moor to the north of the town the bulk of the Scottish army had already crossed the Ribble, while Langton with his 3,000 or 4,000 men remained in Preston as a kind of flank or rearguard. Although several reports had reached him of the proximity of the enemy he appears to have been under the impression that Cromwell had divided his force with the aim of halting Hamilton in Manchester or even that he would only have to deal with the Lancashire militia. Langdale's troops were strung across a narrow lane amidst hedges and ditches. Thus it was essentially an infantry battle which took place, and lasted for four hours. Slowly Langdale's men were pushed back and eventually the Parliamentarian horse thrust their way into the lane to occupy Preston town.

The Duke of Hamilton himself had fought bravely in the battle, but he had left it too late to recall any except a few Scottish lancers to reinforce Langdale. The Scots continued their way southwards through the mud and rain losing stragglers on the road as Cromwell pursued them after the victory. 'The faint and weary soldiers' who 'lagged behind,' wrote a Scottish officer, 'we never saw again'. They even had to abandon much of their ammunition; they did not dare to make a stand, but after another night march on 18/19 August they aimed to reach Warrington in Lancashire where they hoped to confront their pursuers along the line of the River Mersey. But Cromwell trapped them at Winwick, three miles north of Warrington, where after a vain stand the Scots lost many killed or taken prisoner. Later that day the remains of the Scottish infantry surrendered at Warrington. The Scottish cavalry rode on towards Chester

The two sides of a gold twenty-shilling piece, minted at Pontefract Castle during the siege which lasted from June 1648 until March 1649. This particular coin is unique: struck after the King's execution in January, it is inscribed 'Carol⁵ II' for Charles II, and bears a legend around the castle stating that it was minted 'after the death of the father, for the son'.

and North Wales, but finally Lambert caught up with them on 25 August at Uttoxeter in Staffordshire, where Hamilton himself surrendered. Meanwhile Cromwell had mopped up the stragglers and compelled Monro and his men from Ireland to retreat hastily into Scotland where they met a grim fate. By the first week of October Cromwell, having secured the vital towns of Carlisle and Berwick, was himself in Scotland. He had little difficulty in coming to terms with Argyll, who had been opposed to the enterprise of Hamilton and his Engagers. In Edinburgh it was readily agreed that the Engagers should be removed from all offices of trust; Cromwell left Lambert with two regiments as a kind of miniature army of occupation north of the Tweed.

The story of the siege of Colchester, as related by Matthew Carter who took part in it as the King's Quartermaster-General, reveals the loyalty that King Charles I could still inspire. The five hundred men who after many adventures had escaped from Maidstone and patiently awaited the return of their Commander-in-

The 'Old Siege House', Colchester, one of a group of half-timbered houses which stood at the extreme eastern edge of town, outside the walls and near the bridge where Fairfax's siege-works met the River Colne (visible in the plan, *opposite*). The shot-scars in its left-hand wall have been carefully preserved through later centuries.

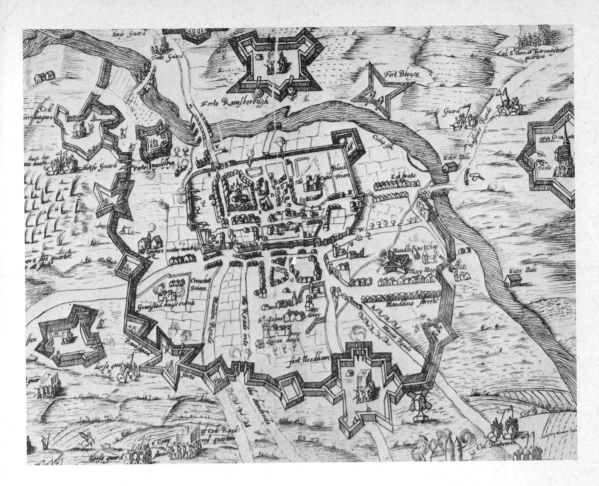

Chief, the Earl of Norwich, from the east of London, were joined at Chelmsford in Essex by a party of fifty gentlemen who had met at Hyde Park Corner and marched through the night by way of Epping having lost only one man and one horse, both of whom were later recovered. Then after collecting arms and provisions they linked up with the Royalists of Essex, whereby, wrote Carter, 'there was Unity of the Engagement, as well as of Interest, and the greater Hopes of Success'. All told, this Royalist force numbered some 4,000 men. On 13 June it was learnt that Fairfax with 5,000 men was hard on their heels when they made what was intended to be only a temporary halt in Colchester. The Parliamentarian army thrust its way through one of the city gates counting on a quick victory as at Maidstone, but was eventually driven out with the loss of 700 men; they left, wrote Carter, 'their Bodies in the Streets and Hedges, as infallible witnesses of what had been done; yawning out their Souls to receive their Arrears in another World, for their religious rebellion in this'. Impressed by his casualties, Thomas Fairfax decided to subject the town to a regular siege, building lines of circumvallation and aiming to starve the garrison into surrender.

A detail from a plan of the siege of Colchester, which ended in the town's surrender to Fairfax on 27 August 1648. On all but the river side Parliamentarian siege-works surround the town, still largely contained within its medieval walls. Buildings outside the walls suffered heavily; disastrously for the besieged, they included the town waterworks and mills (two watermills are shown on the river, to the east).

153

An able group of Royalist officers, including Lord Norwich, Sir Charles Lucas, an Essex man, Sir George Lisle and Lord Capel, organized the defence. Though undertaking one sally to relieve the pressure, the besieged were gradually hemmed in. Most of the mills used to grind corn for bread were destroyed; on 20 July the garrison started eating their horses; later they consumed the cats and dogs in the town. To begin with, all the courtesies were observed, but propaganda was employed. As soon as the news of Cromwell's victory at Preston was known to them, the council of war in Colchester decided to surrender on stiff terms. The rank-and-file were promised 'fair quarter' but the officers had to 'surrender to mercy'. Provoked by such a long resistance, Fairfax and his council of war decided as 'some satisfaction of military justice' to shoot two Royalist officers, Sir Charles Lucas, who had been the soul of the defence, and Sir George Lisle. It is likely that Colonel Henry Ireton, who had taken part in the siege and was one of the three officers who witnessed the shooting, inspired the decision, for he was a stern man. But it was Fairfax's responsibility. Lucas and Lisle paid for their loyalty with their lives. It was not a deed done in hot blood, such as was to be performed at Drogheda in Ireland when the garrison refused to surrender after a breach had been blown in the walls, nor at that stage was it likely to offer a terrible example in order to bring about a speedy ending to the war, for the war had already been won. Twelve years later Fairfax himself was to take up arms in order to restore the King to his throne.

As soon as the second civil war finished Parliament, reinforced by men like Denzil Holles, who had earlier fled to France to avoid the wrath of the army, decided to repeal the vote of no addresses and to reopen negotiations with the King in the Isle of Wight. A commission, consisting chiefly of members of the old peace party and moderates, met Charles at Newport, the capital of the Isle of Wight, and entered upon leisurely discussions. But many men inside and outside the army were no longer disposed to trust the King once he had called in the Scottish Engagers. Petitions were sent to London from the counties seeking 'impartial justice' on all concerned with launching the second civil war. Charles recognized the danger of his position; he agreed at last that Parliament should control the armed forces for twenty years; but he still would not accept a permanent Presbyterian establishment for the English Church.

Meanwhile a republican movement was growing. Colonel Edmund Ludlow, who was one of its protagonists, went to see Fairfax at Colchester early in September to complain to him about the reopening of negotiations with the King. Fairfax was non-committal. Ludlow was received more sympathetically by Ireton. The proposal that came to be adumbrated was to purge Parliament of the peace party or even forcibly to dissolve it. Ireton, dissatisfied with Fairfax, thought of resigning from the army and at the end of the month he resumed his seat in the Commons. But he soon realized

Opposite: the execution of Sir Charles Lucas and Sir George Lisle at Colchester, from a Royalist pamphlet. When Lucas fell, writes Gardiner, 'Lisle, starting forward, caught in his arms the body of his slaughtered friend'. He then took up his station, 'and called to the firing-party to come nearer. "I'll warrant you, sir," said one of the men, "we'll hit you."' Thinking of past battles, he smilingly replied, 'Friends, I have been nearer you when you have missed me.'

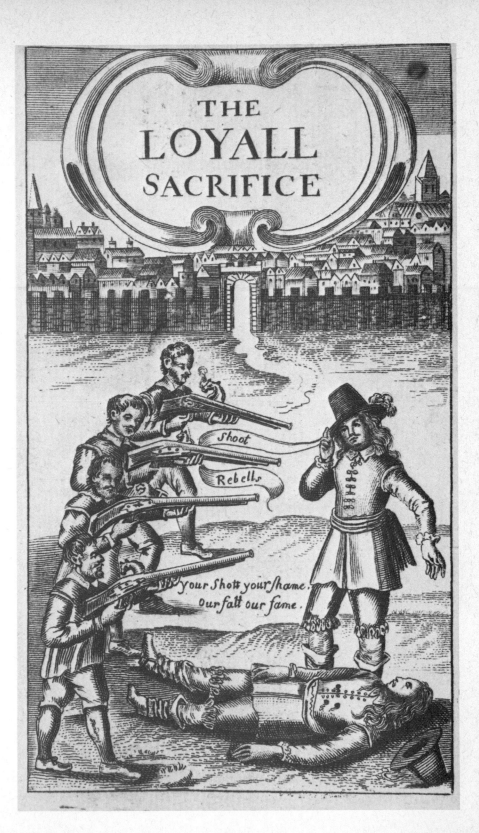

The King and Commissioners from Parliament meeting at Newport in 1648. The text accompanying this woodcut is that of an agreement reached in October; but by then it was too late for agreements, and Parliament was ruled by the army.

that if he wanted to stop the negotiations with the King, he must exert his influence with Fairfax and the army rather than deliver speeches at Westminster. Therefore he drew up a long 'remonstrance' which he wanted the army to submit to Parliament asking for constitutional reforms and demanding that in order to ensure the safety of the people as a whole the King should be brought to trial. At the same time Ireton's and other regiments were seeking 'impartial justice' and the immediate dissolution of Parliament. Ireton tried to make the remonstrance palatable to the Levellers, although they afterwards claimed that they did not want the King to be put on trial before a new constitution had been agreed upon.

King Charles at his trial in January 1649, painted by Edward Bower. The horror which many of his subjects felt at the proceedings was expressed by an officer in a letter to Fairfax: 'I never heard of any throne erected on earth either by God or men for the judging of a king, until the erecting of this late tribunal at Westminster.' On 27 January he asked before sentence was pronounced to be heard before the Lords and Commons, but this was refused. 'I am not suffered to speak,' were his last words at the trial; 'expect what justice other people will have.'

However the council of officers meeting at St Albans on 18 November accepted the remonstrance in principle. Captain (formerly Cornet) Joyce went up to Yorkshire to see Cromwell and bring him the news of the grave decision taken at St Albans.

Both Cromwell and Fairfax were carried along by the tide. Fairfax was reluctantly convinced that the King must be deposed and he led his army into London to coerce Parliament for a second time. Cromwell would have preferred to induce the House of Commons to change its mind about negotiating further with the King rather than expel the members of the peace party there. But Ireton and Ludlow, together with Colonel Pride, a former brewer, thought differently. When the Commons had refused to hear the army's remonstrance and voted in effect to go on treating with the King, these officers carried out a 'purge'. Forty-five members of parliament were put under arrest and 186 others, who had voted in favour of continuing the Newport negotiations, were secluded from the House. It was this purged House of Commons which voted in December that the negotiations at Newport were 'highly dishonour-able and destructive of the peace of the kingdom' and which ten days later appointed a committee to consider how to 'proceed by way of justice' against the King. On 1 January 1649 an ordinance was passed by the Commons instituting a high court specifically to try the King. On 27 January 1649 Charles was condemned to death by sixty-eight members of the court as a tyrant and a traitor who had shed the blood of his own people. In addressing the monarch, who was sentenced to death, the President of the court, John Bradshaw, asserted that the King was subject to the law and that the law proceeded from Parliament. But Charles remained adamant to the

Opposite above: a facsimile of the King's death-warrant. The signatures include Bradshaw's and Cromwell's in the first column, and Ireton's and Mauleverer's in the second. *Below right:* a Flemish painting commemorating the execution of the King, outside the Banqueting House in Whitehall. The executioner, in the medallion top right, has been given the features of Sir Thomas Fairfax. *Below:* Milton's justification of the trial and execution.

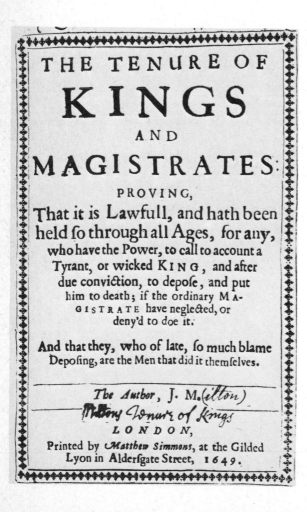

THE TENURE OF
KINGS
AND
MAGISTRATES:
PROVING,
That it is Lawfull, and hath been
held so through all Ages, for any,
who have the Power, to call to account a
Tyrant, or wicked KING, and after
due conviction, to depose, and put
him to death; if the ordinary MA-
GISTRATE have neglected, or
deny'd to doe it.

And that they, who of late, so much blame
Deposing, are the Men that did it themselves.

The Author, J. M. (ilton)
Miltons Tenure of Kings
LONDON,
Printed by *Matthew Simmons*, at the Gilded
Lyon in Aldersgate Street, 1649.

end. Speaking to the group round the scaffold in Whitehall three days later he said:

> Truly I desire their [the people's] liberty and freedom as much as anybody whomsoever; but I must tell you their liberty and freedom consists in having of government those laws by which their life and their goods may be most their own. It is not for having a share in government. . . .

Though he was then beheaded, the Stuart dynasty was not destroyed. During the first week of February the Prince of Wales, now nineteen years old, who was safely in Holland, was told the news of his father's execution and assumed the title of King Charles II. Owing to the unscrupulous methods he used to regain his throne a third civil war came about.

Chapter Eight

THE THIRD CIVIL WAR 1649–1651

Charles II and his exiled Court had now to decide how to overthrow the 'Free Commonwealth', or rather republic, which was in the process of being established in England after the execution of the martyred monarch, and thus to regain the throne of the Stuarts in the Palace of Whitehall. Three possible courses presented themselves. The first was to rely on foreign help. Charles II was an honoured guest in Holland where his brother-in-law, William II, was Stadholder and Captain-General. So long as he could maintain his authority and influence the Dutch Prince would give every assistance

Charles II dancing with his sister Mary at a ball at The Hague. In the background Queen Henrietta Maria and Queen Elizabeth of Bohemia look on; the boy with them is the future William III.

he could to the exiled King. But William quarrelled with the Regents of Amsterdam and soon afterwards died of smallpox, leaving a posthumous child as his heir. Thus the United Netherlands came to be ruled by an oligarchy, just as England was, for the remnants of the victorious House of Commons had assumed full sovereign rights. Other monarchs expressed their sympathies for Charles II, doling out small sums of money as tokens of concern. But though Charles's mother was the aunt of Louis XIV the French Regency had its hands full with a civil war of its own as well as a war with Spain, while the Spaniards, fearful of English naval might, were the first to recognize the Commonwealth Government. So in fact no immediate aid of any significance was available to the Royalists from European Powers.

The second possibility open to Charles II was an invasion of England from Ireland and the third was an invasion from Scotland. The Royalists still living in England were crushed, mulcted with heavy fines and depressed after the second civil war, their activities being closely watched by the county committees. However it was reasonable to suppose that if an invading army arrived by sea or by land they would again rally to the cause. The difficulty here was that both the Irish and the Scots were divided among themselves. It is true that a fortnight before the execution of Charles I the devoted Marquis of Ormonde, the King's Lord-Lieutenant, had succeeded in concluding a treaty at Kilkenny between the Royalists and the Supreme Council of the Confederate Irish by which in return for the grant of the free exercise of Roman Catholicism and the independence of the Irish Parliament the confederates promised to supply Ormonde with an army of over 15,000 men. Thus the Lord-Lieutenant might hope to wipe out such few soldiers loyal to the English Parliament as there were in Ireland and to convert the island into a base from which England could be invaded. That this was a practical policy was indicated by the ease with which six months earlier Colonel George Monro had been able to land troops from Ulster in western Scotland to join in the disastrous Preston campaign. The Scots for their part were divided between the Covenanters who looked to the astute and pious Argyll for leadership, the surviving Engagers whose heads, the second Duke of Hamilton and the Earl of Lauderdale, had been banished after the campaign of 1648 and were now with Charles II in exile, and the Royalists, mainly concentrated in the Highlands, whose hero was the Marquis of Montrose.

The Covenanters, angry with an English Parliament for having had the impertinence to execute a Scottish monarch, proclaimed Charles II as King on 5 February 1649. On 22 February Charles appointed Montrose as his Captain-General in Scotland with instructions to form the nucleus of an army with which to recruit the Highland clans. But Charles's immediate hopes were fixed on Ireland; even before his father's death Ormonde had invited him to

Opposite: a proclamation dated 1 February 1649 acknowledging Prince Charles, 'next heire of the blood Royall to his Father King Charls (whose late wicked and trayterous murther wee doe from our soules abominate, and all parties and consenters thereunto) to be by hereditary Birthright, and lawful succession, rightful and undoubted King of Great Britain, France and Ireland.'

A
PROCLAMATION
PROCLAMING
CHARLS
Prince of Wales, King of Great
Brittaine, France, and Ireland.

WEE the Noblemen, Judges, Knights, Lawyers, Gentlemen, Freeholders, Merchants,
Citizens, Yeomen, Seamen, and other free-
men of England, doe, according to our Allegiance and Covenant, by these presents hartily,
joyfully and unanimously acknowledg and proclaime the Illustrious Charls Prince of Wales, next heire of the blood Royall to
his Father King Charls (whose late wicked and trayterous murther
wee doe from our soules abominate, and all parties and consenters thereunto) to be by hereditary Birthright, and lawfull succession, rightfull and undoubted King of Great Brittaine, France
and Ireland, and the Dominions thereunto belonging. And that wee
will faithfully, constantly and sinceerely in our severall places and
callings defend and maintaine his Royall Person, Crowne, and
Dignity with our Estates, Lives, and last drop of our bloods,
against all opposers thereof; whom wee doe hereby declare to bee
Traytors and Enemies to his Majesty and his Kingdoms. In
testimony whereof, wee have caused these to be published and proclaimed throughout al Counties and Corporations of this Realm,
the first day of February in the first yeare of his Majesties Raigne.
God save KING CHARLS the Second.

come there so that he might direct an invasion of England. But it was not until the middle of September that Charles reached Jersey in preparation for going on to Ireland. Ormonde had again urged him to come since he was aware that the confederate Irish were more concerned with securing their own liberties than with actually assisting the King. Ormonde thought that only the presence of Charles in Dublin would unite the Irish in his cause. In fact by the time Charles was ready to land there it was too late: knowing what was on foot, the English Parliament persuaded Oliver Cromwell to go to Ireland as its Lord-Lieutenant and Captain-General to punish the native Irish for their rebellion in 1641 and to overthrow the Royalists there. Even before Cromwell's arrival with a well-paid and well-provisioned army Ormonde's troops had been defeated at the battle of Rathmines near Dublin (2 August 1649), while on 3 September Cromwell crushed and largely slaughtered the garrison of the key town of Drogheda in Leinster which consisted partly of Royalists and partly of native Irish. While Charles was in Jersey Cromwell subdued much of Munster, the principal home of Irish Royalists. Ormonde wrote to the King telling him that without considerable sums of money he could not raise another army after

Charles II with the Scottish Commissioners at Breda in 1650.

THE SCOTS HOLDING THEIR YOVNG KINGES NOSE TO Y GRINSTONE

Come to the Grinstone Charles tis now to late.
To Recolect tis presbiterian fate..

You Covnant pretenders must shee
The Subiect of your Tradgie Comedie

Jockie

Stoope Charles

A cartoon from a broadsheet of 1651 attacks both the Scots and Charles II, whom it sees as taking advantage of each other – Charles by feigning sympathy for the Presbyterian Kirk, the Scots by using Charles as an excuse to invade England.

these defeats nor advise Charles to continue on his way from Jersey. The fact that substantial numbers of Englishmen fighting in Ireland had changed sides to enlist in Cromwell's army, while the native Irish were terrified, revealed that the hope of restoring the King to his throne in England with the help of a combined Irish army was negligible.

After learning the bad news from Ireland Charles left Jersey in February 1650. The victorious Parliamentarian commander returned to London at the end of May, leaving an army of occupation under the command of his son-in-law, Ireton. The King now felt that he had no alternative but to listen to the stringent terms which the Scots required him to accept before they would allow him to come to Scotland. When in March 1649 Commissioners had arrived in Holland to see their new King, he had refused to commit himself to them and played for time, hoping for a victory in Ireland and help from Montrose. Now, a year later, Charles entered into negotiations with fresh Scottish Commissioners who met him at Breda. The Committee of Estates, which ruled Scotland, insisted upon stiff and uncompromising terms; even Argyll thought that they went too far. But Charles was pressed by his brother-in-law William II to agree to them. After six weeks of arguing and diplomatic manœuvring he signed on 1 May 1650 a draft agreement known as the Treaty of Breda. By this Charles in effect promised to swear to the two Covenants, which committed him to impose a Presbyterian system on England as well as Scotland, to recognize the legality of the purged Scottish Parliament, to repudiate his arrangements with Ormonde and Montrose and to forbid the exercise of the Roman Catholic religion anywhere in his dominions. In return all that the Scottish Commissioners offered was formally to invite Charles to Scotland to be crowned King and to give verbal assurances that the Engagers would be restored at least to their personal rights as subjects. The Commissioners did not really trust Charles to fulfil all his promises, but they believed they had him in a cleft stick. A well-informed reporter at Breda thought that on one side the King would never 'prove a strenuous defender of their [the Scottish] faith', while on the other the Scots at heart hated monarchy and merely intended to use Charles as a figurehead for their own ends. Thus the Covenanters neither then nor after Charles's arrival in Scotland on 23 June committed themselves to fighting for his restoration to the English throne. Yet it was because Charles reluctantly went to Scotland that the third civil war came about.

The very day after Charles landed the Council of State in London debated the question whether in the interests of the security of the Commonwealth Scotland should be invaded by an English army. It has to be remembered that although England and Scotland have now been politically united as one kingdom for over 250 years, in the mid-seventeenth century the Scots were regarded by the English not as fellow subjects of the Stuarts but as national enemies. Only two years earlier a Scots army had invaded England in an attempt to restore a Scots king to power there. The Council of State therefore decided to launch a preventive war by ordering Lord Fairfax to lead an army into Scotland; for the majority of the members were convinced that if that were not done a Scots army, headed by Charles II, would be crossing the northern frontier. They were both right and wrong; for while Charles was in fact to move into England in the following year, in the summer of 1650 Argyll and the dominant Covenanters had no intention of doing so. Fairfax demurred. He said if the Scots attacked England he would lay down his life in opposing them, but he refused to make war on a people between whom and the English Parliament there still existed a Solemn League and Covenant; the Councillors were not unduly concerned over subtle differences between the Scottish Covenanters and the Scottish Engagers. But Fairfax was adamant in refusing the command; Cromwell, who had returned from Ireland in the third week of May, was appointed in his place.

It is often assumed that Fairfax was a softer and milder character than Cromwell. But in fact his shooting of the two knights at Colchester in 1648 and the fierceness with which he suppressed army mutinies in 1649 show that he was stern and tough. He had refused to take any oath to the Commonwealth which would have meant giving his approval to the trial and execution of Charles I. Under the influence of his wife, who was both Presbyterian and Royalist, Fairfax was becoming alienated from the new régime and glad to

Castrum puellarum

wash his hands of it. Cromwell therefore on 22 July led an army of some 16,000 men over the Tweed; by the middle of August he was attempting to surround and cut off Edinburgh. The war of manœuvre – Cromwell was opposed by a large Covenanting army under David Leslie, who had fought with him at Marston Moor – was accompanied by a war of propaganda. Cromwell claimed that by welcoming the light-hearted Charles II into their bosoms the Scots were fighting against 'the very power of godliness and holiness'. To this the Scots retorted by obliging Charles to declare that his father had been guilty in resisting the reformation of the Church of England and that his mother was an idolatress. Thus Charles too became godly and holy. However he remarked in confidence that he remained at heart a true child of the Anglican Church and a true Cavalier. Indeed he used every resource and any lie to rekindle the civil wars.

On 3 September Cromwell won a major victory over the Scots at Dunbar. Anxious to prove that they were fighting for their religion and their country rather than in the cause of 'a malignant king', Commissioners for Purging appointed by the Committee of

Edinburgh, occupied by Cromwell in December 1650 after the battle of Dunbar. On the left is the castle, on its hill; in the centre St Giles's Cathedral, scene of the riot against Charles I's proposed prayer book (*see* p. 41); Holyrood Palace lies away to the right, out of the picture.

An engraving of the battle
of Dunbar, 3 September
1650. Cromwell's troops
have left their camp (far
right); some are still crossing
the steep glen leading down
to the sea. At the far left, the
English cavalry meet the
Scottish right wing, in a
burst of gunfire; in the
centre left, pikemen of the
two sides are in action; just
above the glen the cavalry of
the Scottish left wing are
routed and flee up the hill,
leaving their devastated
camp.

et Hiberniæ PROTECTORI præpotentisimo F.F. Fælicitatem, victorias, Triumphos
Militiæ viris Primipilaribus, hanc calcographicam Prælij Dunbarrensis Iconim DDL

Sold by Pet. Stint

One of the medals awarded, on the orders of the House of Commons, to soldiers who had fought at the battle of Dunbar. Cromwell himself suggested the design, which shows him in front of a battlefield with the inscription 'word at Dunbar · The Lord of Hosts': the medallist Thomas Simon was sent to Edinburgh to draw Cromwell from life.

Estates were expelling unpurified (and experienced) soldiers from Leslie's army up to the eve of the battle. Furthermore Leslie was induced through the influence of the Kirk to move his army off the impregnable position it had taken up on Doon Hill, two miles from the port of Dunbar, which was the English base, forward on to the rich sloping grasslands below the line of the Lammermuir Hills so as to be able to fall like Ehud upon the Moabites.

Observing this, Cromwell and his fellow generals decided to attack at dawn on the following day the new strung-out Scottish position stretching from the hills down towards the sea. This involved one of the hardest manœuvres in war, an attack beginning in the dark, preceded by the crossing of a natural obstacle, in this case a steep and slippery glen or trough which protected the Scottish right. What it did not involve, as has often been asserted, was an attack directed mainly by English infantrymen on the Scottish cavalry which formed the right flank of their long line. Cromwell knew better than any man that except in wooded country pikemen and musketeers stood little chance against mounted and armoured men. The assault was launched against the Scottish right by six cavalry regiments led by Major-General Lambert and Lieutenant-General Fleetwood, while Colonel Monck with a brigade of foot attacked the Scottish infantry in the centre. The Scots were by no means completely surprised, but after a night spent without cover in wet cornfields they were somewhat demoralized. Nevertheless, as Cromwell was to report, 'the enemy made a gallant resistance, and there was a very hot dispute at sword's point between our horse and theirs'. Cromwell then sent in his reserves – his own regiment of horse and three regiments of foot. The foot regiments repulsed the finest of the Scottish infantry at push of pike, while the cavalry helped to rout Leslie's right wing. After stiff resistance on their right

Charles II was crowned at the traditional Scottish coronation place of Scone on 1 January 1651 (*below*). *Right:* the reverse of a medal struck to commemorate the event; it bears the lion and thistle and the Scottish motto *Nemo me impune lacessit* – 'No one shall provoke me with impunity'.

The Marquis of Montrose (*see* p. 90) had returned to Scotland after Charles I's death to fight for his son, but he was betrayed and executed as a traitor in Edinburgh in 1650. This engraving shows him being cut down from the gallows and, on the right, being beheaded and quartered.

and centre the Scots panicked and threw down their arms and their left wing, hemmed in at the base of the hills where it had been contained by a mere demonstration, disintegrated. The English took 10,000 prisoners, about half of the Scottish army, and killed 3,000 while their own losses were small. This battle was not strictly part of the third civil war, for it was a national conflict, but because of it the young King was able, after he had been crowned at Scone on 1 January 1651, to revive Scottish Royalism and meld it with that of English sympathizers in the north to engage on one last great battle between Cavaliers and Roundheads.

Charles's aim – ever since that fatal day when he left Holland only to learn on his way of the defeat of his most gallant and loyal Scots follower, Montrose, cruelly hanged and quartered as a traitor – had been to unite all his supporters in Scotland and England to fight together for his restoration. The overthrow of the Covenanter army at Dunbar gave Charles his opportunity, although it was not until

2 June 1651 that the Act of Classes which prevented the former Engagers from serving in the army was repealed by the Scottish Parliament. Meanwhile every effort had been exerted to revive the flame of Royalism in England. The country was divided into districts in which Royalist organizers began secret preparations. In Norfolk a premature rising had taken place before Christmas; a scheme was worked out for a landing at Dover Castle: in Lancashire Royalists were promised Scottish help if they could arouse the country gentry, reputedly the most Royalist in England, on behalf of the King. The second Duke of Buckingham was provided with the nucleus of an army which it was hoped could be enlisted in the north-west and in North Wales. By this time many English Presbyterians were beginning to opt for monarchy. Had not Charles I offered to accept a Presbyterian Church while he was in the Isle of Wight? Had not the Presbyterian commanders like Essex and Manchester always been as loyal to the monarchy as to Parliament? A Presbyterian minister rejoicing in the name of Love was arrested in London during May for conspiring on behalf of the King. He and another minister were executed on Tower Hill at the beginning of August as a warning to all other Presbyterians actually sympathetic to Charles II.

Though the republican authorities throughout his southern kingdom were sufficiently watchful to prevent any serious risings unless and until Charles won a victory on English soil, in Scotland the King was at last supreme. He was accepted as nominal Commander-in-Chief of the Scottish army, while the sinister Marquis of Argyll, who had changed sides once too often, pleading his wife's illness retired in dudgeon to his Highland castle of Inverary. The winter put an end to hostilities. Leslie with the remains of his army, now gradually reinforced by Engagers and Royalist Highlanders, defied the English south of Stirling and along the line of the River Forth. Cromwell had made one or two attempts to outflank him both to the east and to the west of Stirling, but to no avail. The English Commander-in-Chief himself was taken ill in the course of an inclement winter and blustery spring, so that it was not until June that campaigning was vigorously resumed. On 17 July Colonel Robert Overton with a force of 1,600 men managed to cross the Forth by boats from South Queensferry to North Queensferry (where the old Forth Bridge was later to be built). Lambert then followed him across with a larger force and defeated a Scottish detachment which was sent to deal with him at the battle of Inverkeithing on 20 July. Thereupon Cromwell carried his whole army except for four cavalry and four infantry regiments across the river and made for Perth, thus cutting the lines of communication of the Scots army. The Scots now had two alternatives if they were not to be surrounded – to fight where they stood or to march into England so as to sever Cromwell's own communications with the south. Understandably Charles II resolved on the latter alternative, which

William Hamilton, second Duke of Hamilton (1616–51), leader of the Engagers. The exclusion of Engagers from the Royalist army was repealed in June 1651, and Hamilton supported Charles II's plan to invade England. He died of wounds received at the battle of Worcester.

was approved by the leader of the Engagers, the second Duke of Hamilton, but not apparently by Leslie, who had so skilfully withstood Cromwell at Stirling. Charles hoped that once in England Royalists there would again rally to his side. That was why he chose the route through Carlisle, Warrington and Manchester where Royalism was still thought to be strong.

It has been said that the Scots army was less well trained and less adequately armed than the English. It is not clear why this should have been so once all the Scots were permitted to serve the King, unless it was because the kingdom was poorer than England. But what is certain is that the hearts of many of the Scots who marched across the border – covering three hundred miles in three weeks – were not in the campaign; this was particularly true of Leslie who made gloomy prognostications *en route*. The size of this army is variously estimated: it may have been only just over 13,000 men. On the other hand, Cromwell's army had been reinforced since Dunbar, while Major-General Thomas Harrison commanded a cavalry force which had long been stationed near the border ready to repel invasion. The militiamen of the threatened northern counties were called up and Fleetwood had been sent south to collect a fresh army there. Cromwell tried to soothe fearful politicians in London by saying that they might have to suffer 'some inconveniences' but that his crossing of the Forth had been the only method of avoiding another year's campaign in Scotland.

Charles II's hopes of assistance from English Royalists – both Anglicans and Presbyterians – were dashed. The Earl of Derby had arrived from the Isle of Man to try to inspirit Lancashire, but Lancastrians had no reason to love the Scots. On 25 August Derby's small force was defeated at Wigan by a cavalry regiment under Colonel Robert Lilburne (brother of the Leveller leader, Freeborn John) and Derby himself fled to join the King. A Scottish general, the Earl of Middleton, was unsuccessful with recruiting in Wales. However Charles's army managed to brush aside a cavalry army commanded by Harrison and Lambert, who had been sent ahead by Cromwell, and finally reached Worcester exhausted on 22 August. Charles was delighted to be greeted with a warm welcome from the Mayor, whom he knighted, and on Sunday 24 August was able to listen to an Anglican sermon preached in the cathedral. Yet few Midland Royalists came to his help, for they too were alienated by the Scots.

James Stanley, Earl of Derby (1607–51), tried to raise Lancashire in support of the King but was defeated at Wigan in August 1651. He too fought at Worcester, where he was captured, and was later executed. He was the husband of the Countess who defended Lathom House (p. 93).

Cromwell had more than 28,000 men at his disposal when he caught up with Charles at Worcester. So he was able almost to surround the city. Fleetwood was put in command of a force which was instructed to ford the River Teme, a tributary of the Severn, and attack three fine Scottish regiments which were deployed south of the city. Cromwell placed his cannon to the east, intending, it seems, to attack the walled city simultaneously on two fronts. As at Dunbar, he assumed command of a reserve, consisting of his life-

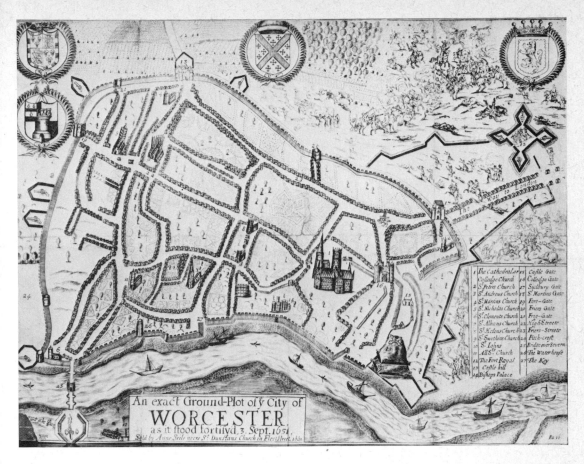

An exact Ground-Plot of ỹ City of
WORCESTER
as it ſtood fortifyd, 3. Sept. 1651.
Sold by Anne Seile neere St Dunstans Church in Fleetstreet. 1660.

1 The Cathedral or	15 Castle Gate
Colledge Church	16 Colledge Gate
2 St Peters Church	17 Sydbury Gate
3 St Andrews Church	18 St Martins Gate
4 St Martins Church	19 Fore-Gate
5 St Nicholas Church	20 Friers Gate
6 St Clements Church	21 Frog-Gate
7 St Albans Church	22 High Streete
8 St Helens Church	23 Friers-Streete
9 St Swithins Church	24 Pitch-croft
10 St Johns	25 Bridge over Severn
11 Alls.. Church	26 The Waterhouse
12 The Fort Royal	27 The Key
13 Castle hill	
14 Bishops Palace	

guards, his own regiment of horse, and two experienced infantry regiments, so that when Fleetwood was held up in crossing the Teme Oliver was able to relieve the pressure on his second-in-command by throwing a bridge of boats over the Severn, he himself leading his men across. Charles II, who could watch the operations from the cathedral tower, tried to attack the Parliamentarian artillery positions by a sortie uphill to the east of the city. The struggle lasted three hours. Eventually the defenders of Worcester were overwhelmed. Four thousand Scots who had taken little part in the battle were pursued, cut off, and taken prisoner before they could flee for home. Oliver Cromwell described the victory as 'a crowning mercy'. One of his chaplains, Hugh Peter, observed to the English militia who had fought in the battle: 'When your wives and children shall ask you where you have been, and what news: say you have been at Worcester, where England's sorrows began, and where they are happily ended.' For the first skirmish in the civil wars had been fought by Prince Rupert against Fiennes's men near Worcester almost precisely nine years earlier.

After Worcester another symbolic and romantic episode took place. Charles II himself, who had fought bravely until the very last,

'Worcester as it stood fortify'd, 3. Sept. 1651'. The battle was fought to the east of the city, though near enough for Charles II to watch it from the cathedral tower. The Royalists attempted to attack Cromwell's position on the hill. When they were defeated neither the city nor Fort Royal – upper right – could hold out.

showing, it was said, 'much steadiness of mind and undaunted courage', succeeded after forty-five days of adventure, eluding every Roundhead soldier who would have liked to take him prisoner to reap a reward, in escaping across the sea to France. Almost everywhere he went he found loyal subjects to help him on his way. During these weeks he learned much about his countrymen and about their devotion to their religion, less ostentatious and less hypocritical, it seemed to him, than that of the overtly pious Scots. It was these ancient loyalties that in the end were to bring him back to his father's throne.

What were the consequences of these civil wars? If the events of 1641–42 constituted the eruption of the first English revolution, a second revolution had taken place in 1648 when the House of Commons was purged of those members who still wanted to come to an agreement with the King and to transform him into a constitutional monarch. It is fascinating to contemplate what might have happened if the 'purged' members had had their way. For the remainder of his life Charles I might have been the same kind of figurehead that King Frederick I of Sweden was to be in the eighteenth century. A bigoted and exclusive Presbyterian Church, similar to the Scottish Kirk, might have been set up instead of the latitudinarian Anglican establishment which has endured until the present day. But what in fact happened was that Charles I was tried and executed, his son was comprehensively defeated in the third

Boscobel House, Shropshire. After the battle of Worcester Charles II lay in hiding here for two days, one of them spent in the famous oak tree.

civil war, and two years later General Oliver Cromwell became Lord Protector of the Commonwealth.

Cromwell was not a dictator; he was required to accept the advice of his Council of State; moreover parliaments of one kind or another sat sporadically until the close of the Interregnum. Cromwell, however, was a strong man, a born leader, and a tolerant ruler. He allowed Jews to return to England; he permitted Roman Catholics and Anglicans to worship privately in London; and although he instituted a State Church with Triers and Ejectors instead of bishops and deans, he did not interfere with eccentric Christian sects so long as they behaved themselves. After his death anarchy broke loose. His son Richard was an ineffective Protector while the leading generals, Fleetwood, Lambert and Monck, quarrelled among themselves. So the realists throughout the country came to the conclusion that a return to monarchy was the only sure road to domestic peace.

The Great Seal of England used by the Commonwealth in 1651 shows the House of Commons in session in 'the third year of freedom', with the Speaker in the chair, two clerks writing at the table on which the mace is laid, and a member addressing the House. In 1648 those members who favoured an accommodation with Charles had been expelled, leaving the 'Rump'; in another two years even that would prove too much for Cromwell, and 'freedom', in the sense of parliamentary government, would disappear.

The civil wars had three main results. The first was that the feudal rights of the Crown and the Tudor prerogative courts, which Charles I had agreed to abolish in 1641, were never to be restored. Secondly, the King's power to levy taxes without the consent of Parliament or to arrest members of the House of Commons without showing cause was destroyed. Lastly, because Parliament won the civil wars, Parliament henceforward became an unchallengeable part of the British constitution. Both Charles II and his brother, James II, dreaded a renewal of civil wars. Charles, being more astute than his brother, prevented the outbreak of civil war during the 'exclusionist crisis' and the Whig plotting of 1678–83. James, when his subjects rebelled against him in 1688 with the invaluable assistance of his nephew and son-in-law, William III of Orange, fled first from his army headquarters at Salisbury and then from his capital rather than fight it out. Since then, up to the time of writing, there have been no more civil wars in Great Britain.

BIBLIOGRAPHY

In this bibliography I confine myself chiefly to secondary authorities because the original authorities, ranging from news-letters to memoirs, are numberless. Some of the more important primary authorities are listed in Young and Holmes (IV, below) and Austin Woolrych (ditto). I include only a few articles in learned journals because they also are so many. The standard bibliography for the subject is *Bibliography of British History Stuart Period 1603–1714* (ed. Godfrey Davies and Mary Frear Keeler, 1970) which discusses the sources for the civil war on pages 225–43; but inevitably it does not contain most of the secondary authorities published since about 1966.

I THE CAUSES OF THE CIVIL WAR

Authorities on this subject may be divided roughly into three parts: (1) those who think that the origins of the civil war were chiefly social and economic, (2) the Marxists, and (3) the traditional liberal political view. Philip A. M. Taylor (ed.), *The Origins of the English Civil War: Conspiracy, Crusade or Class Conflict* (1960), sets out quotations from all these views, but though the editor is self-assured, it is now fifteen years out of date.

For the social and economic interpretation see the following books by Lawrence Stone who is the commander-in-chief in this field: Lawrence Stone (ed.), *Social Change and Revolution in England* (1965), Lawrence Stone, *The Causes of the English Revolution 1529–1642* (1972) and *Crisis of the Aristocracy 1558–1641* (1965). Two articles, R. H. Tawney, 'The Rise of the Gentry' in *Economic History Review* (1941), and Hugh Trevor-Roper, 'The Gentry 1540–1640' in *Economic History Review* (1953), created a sensation in academic circles when they were first published and stimulated a great deal of valuable research, but the controversy is now largely a dead duck.

If Lawrence Stone is c-in-c for the social interpretation of the origins of the civil war, Dr Christopher Hill is the doyen of the Marxist interpretation. See Christopher Hill and E. Dell (eds.), *The Good Old Cause, the English Revolution: its causes, course and consequences* (1949), Christopher Hill (ed.), *The English Revolution* (1955), and Christopher Hill, *Puritanism and Revolution* (1965). See also books and articles by Brian Manning, e.g. 'The Nobles, the People and the Constitution' in *Past and Present* (1956). Critics of the class interpretation (who include myself) rely partly on the analysis of the membership of the House of Commons in D. Brunton and D. H. Pennington, *Members of the Long Parliament* (1954), and Mary

Frear Keeler, *The Long Parliament of 1640–1641* (1954); though the former book has been fiercely attacked by the Marxists it remains pretty convincing.

The best of the other books, written from a moderate point of view, are: Conrad Russell (ed.), *The Origins of the English Civil War* (1973); C. V. Wedgwood, *The King's Peace* (1954); P. Zagorin, 'The Social Interpretation of the English Revolution' in the *Journal of Economic History* (1959) and *The Court and County* (1969). See also J. H. Hexter, 'The Storm over the Gentry' in *Reappraisals in History* (1963).

II GENERAL HISTORY

For the general history of the period during which the civil war originated and was fought, scc S. R. Gardiner, *History of England from the Accession of James I to the Outbreak of the Civil War* (1884), *History of the Great Civil War 1642–1649* (1893) and *History of the Commonwealth and Protectorate* (1903); Ivan Roots, *The Great Rebellion* (now under revision); and C. V. Wedgwood, *The King's War* (1958). See also W. D. Macray (ed.), The Earl of Clarendon, *The History of the Rebellion and the Civil Wars in England* (1888), but it needs to be remembered that Clarendon disliked most military men and is not to be trusted over what he writes about them.

III COUNTY HISTORIES

E. A. Andriette, *Devon and Exeter in the Civil War* (1971); A. R. Bayley, *The Great Civil War in Dorset* (1961); E. Broxap, *The Great Civil War in Lancashire 1642–1651* (1910); J. T. Cliffe, *The Yorkshire Gentry* (1969); Mary Coate, *Cornwall in the Great Civil War and Interregnum 1642–1660* (1963); A. M. Everitt, *The County Committee of Kent in the Civil War* (1957), *Suffolk and the Great Rebellion 1640–1660* (1960) and *The Community of Kent and the Great Rebellion* (1966); W. G. Farrow, *The Civil War in Shropshire* (1926); G. N. Godwin, *The Civil War in Hampshire* (1904); A. Kingston, *Hertfordshire in the Great Civil War* (1894); J. S. Morrill, *Cheshire 1630–1660* (1974); Valerie Pearl, *London on the Outbreak of the Puritan Revolution* (1961); D. H. Pennington and Ivan Roots, *The Committee at Stafford 1643–1645* (1957); B. N. Reckitt, *Charles the First and Hull* (1952); C. T. Sandford, *Sussex in the Great Civil War and Interregnum* (1910); David Underdown, *Somerset in the Civil War and Interregnum* (1973); J. Willis-Bund, *The Civil War in Worcestershire* (1905).

IV MILITARY HISTORY

John Adair, *Roundhead General: a Military Biography of Sir William Waller* (1969) and *Cheriton 1644* (1973); T. S. Baldock, *Cromwell as a Soldier* (1899); F. T. R. Edgar, *Sir Ralph Hopton* (1968); C. H. Firth, *Cromwell's Army* (1962); C. R. Markham, *A Life of the Great Lord Fairfax* (1870); Walter Money, *The First and Second Battles of Newbury* (1881); J. R. Powell, *The Navy in the English Civil War* (1962); H. C. B. Rogers, *Battles and Generals of the Civil Wars* (1968); Peter Wenham, *The Great and Close Siege of York* (1970); Austin Woolrych, *Battles of the Civil War* (1961); Peter Young, *Edgehill 1642* (1967) and *Marston Moor 1644* (1970).

My own accounts of the big battles will be found in Maurice Ashley, *The Greatness of Oliver Cromwell* (revised 1962) and *Cromwell's Generals* (1954).

Peter Young and Ian Roy have written various articles on the Royalist army; Brigadier Young's articles have mostly appeared in the *Journal of the Society for Army Historical Research*. With these should be compared various articles by Godfrey Davies, and C. H. Firth and Godfrey Davies, *The Regimental History of Cromwell's Army* (1940). There is no good book on the Earl of Essex or Prince Rupert, but two are to be published shortly on Rupert, one by Maurice Ashley concentrating on the military aspects, the other a deeply researched life by Patrick Morrah.

While this book was in the press *The English Civil War* by Peter Young and Richard Holmes was published in April 1974; this is largely a revised and expanded version of A. H. Burne and Peter Young, *The Great Civil War* (1959). The first two chapters are somewhat perfunctory in their summary of the origins of the civil war and notice is not always taken of the criticisms of the earlier book by Austin Woolrych, David Underdown and others.

LIST OF ILLUSTRATIONS

Sir Peter Paul Rubens, 1625. Albertina, Vienna. *Photo Bildarchiv der Österreichisches Nationalbibliothek, Vienna*

27 John Felton; engraving by R. Sawyer, 1628. Ashmolean Museum, Oxford

The raising of the siege of the island of Rhé, 8 November 1627; contemporary oil painting by an unknown French artist. Musée de Versailles. *Photo Giraudon*

28 Engraving from the broadsheet *Popish Plots and Treasons*, 1627. British Museum, London

'Sound-Head, Rattle-Head and Round-Head'; engraving, 1642. British Museum, London

31 Sir John Eliot; oil painting by an unknown artist, said to have been made a few days before Eliot's death in 1632. By kind permission of Lord St Germains. *Photo National Portrait Gallery, London*

33 *The good Fellowes Complaint*; left half of a song-sheet lamenting the excise on liquor, published in London. The Manchester Public Libraries

34 Religious dissenters fleeing from England; woodcut from an early seventeenth-century copy of an Elizabethan ballad, *The most Rare and Excellent History of the Dutchess of Suffolk and her husband Richard Bertie's Calamities*. British Library, London

36 Charles I, Henrietta Maria and their son Prince Charles dining at Whitehall; detail of an oil painting by Joachim Houckgeest, c. 1632–35. By gracious permission of Her Majesty the Queen

37 Title-page of *Dies Dominica*, 1639. British Library, London

38 Silver ampulla used at the coronation of Charles I at Holyrood, Edinburgh, 1633. National Museum of Antiquities of Scotland, Edinburgh

Interior of the Queen's Chapel in St James's Palace, London; by Inigo Jones, 1623–27. By gracious permission of Her Majesty the Queen

39 Charles I with Henrietta Maria and their son Prince Charles; oil painting by Hendrick Gerritszoon Pot, probably painted in 1632. By gracious permission of Her Majesty the Queen

40 Title-page of *The Booke of Common Prayer . . . for the use of the Church of Scotland*, Edinburgh, 1637. British Library, London

41 Riot in St Giles's Cathedral, Edinburgh, during the reading of the new Scottish prayer book, 1637; etching by Wenceslaus Hollar from John Vicars' *Sight of the Transactions of these latter yeares*, 1646. British Library, London

42 James Hamilton, third Marquis and first Duke of Hamilton; detail of an oil painting by Daniel Mytens, 1629. The Duke of Hamilton and Brandon, on loan to the National Gallery of Scotland, Edinburgh. *Photo National Galleries of Scotland*

43 Archibald Campbell, first Marquis of Argyll; oil painting after David Scougall. National Portrait Gallery, London

44 Robert Rich, second Earl of Warwick; detail of a contemporary engraving. British Museum, London

45 Thomas Wentworth, first Earl of Strafford; oil painting, studio of Sir Anthony van Dyck, c. 1633. National Portrait Gallery, London

46 *Platform of the Lower House of this Present Parliament*, 13 April 1640; engraving from a broadsheet British Museum, London

48 Londoners fleeing from the plague; woodcut from a broadsheet entitled *A Looking-glasse for City and Countrey*, London, early seventeenth century. British Museum, London

Two details of a woodcut from a broadsheet entitled *These Tradesmen are Preachers in and about the City of London; or, A Discovery of the most Dangerovs and Damnable Tenets that have been spread within this few yeares: By many Erronious, Heriticall and Mechannick spirits. By which the very foundation of Christian knowledge and practise is endeavoured to be overturned*, Lon-

don, 1647. The confectioner, pounding something in a mortar, is Graunt, the comfit-maker in Bucklersbury, author in 1645 of a tract entitled *Truths Victory against Heresie*; the glove-maker is Richard Rogers, who had a congregation at Blue Anchor Alley in the suburbs of London. British Library, London

49 John Pym; miniature by Samuel Cooper. By courtesy of the Administrative Trustees of the Chequers Trust

51 Sir William Balfour; detail of a contemporary engraving. British Museum, London

52 The impeachment of the Earl of Strafford; etching by Wenceslaus Hollar, 1641. British Museum, London

53 The execution of the Earl of Strafford; etching by Wenceslaus Hollar, 1641. British Museum, London

Unique gold medal commemorating the execution of the Earl of Strafford, 1641; the design is unfinished, being engraved on one side only and without an inscription in the encircling border. British Museum, London. *Photo Ray Gardner*

55 Robert Devereux, third Earl of Essex; oil painting attributed to Daniel Mytens. National Portrait Gallery, London

56 Map of Ireland relating to the rebellion of 1641–42; engraving, c. 1642. British Library, London

57 Title-page of *An Exact and true Relation of the late Plots which were contrived and hatched in Ireland*, London, 1641. British Library, London

58 Hampton Court Palace seen from the River Thames; oil painting by an unknown artist, c. 1640. By gracious permission of Her Majesty the Queen

59 *Colonell Lunsford assaulting the Londoners at Westminster Hall, with a great rout of ruffinly Cavaleires*; etching by Wenceslaus Hollar from John Vicars' *Sight of the Transactions of these latter yeares*, 1646. British Library, London

Edward Sackville, fourth Earl of Dorset; engraving by Robert van Voerst (d. 1635/36). British Museum, London

60 Instructions from Charles I to his Attorney-General, Sir Edward Herbert, concerning the proposed impeachment of the six members of parliament, 3 January 1642. MS. Egerton 2546, f.20. British Library, London

61 Title-page of *Master Pym His Speech in Parliament*, London, 1642. National Portrait Gallery, London

62 William Cavendish, Earl, Marquis and later first Duke of Newcastle; miniature, probably by Samuel Cooper, after a portrait by Sir Anthony van Dyck (d. 1641). Collection of the Duke of Buccleuch and Queensberry. *Photo Victoria and Albert Museum, London*

63 Reverse of a medal struck in Holland to commemorate the arrival of Queen Henrietta Maria; electrotype of a gold medal at The Hague, 1642. British Museum, London. *Photo Ray Gardner*

64 Charles I with Sir Edward Walker; oil painting by an unknown artist. National Portrait Gallery, London

66 Sir Ralph Hopton; detail of an oil painting by an unknown artist, *c.* 1637. National Portrait Gallery, London

Sir William Waller; detail of an oil painting by an unknown artist. National Portrait Gallery, London

67 Destruction of the Cheapside Cross in London in 1643; detail of an etching by Wenceslaus Hollar from John Vicars' *Sight of the Transactions of these latter yeares*, London, 1646. The accompanying text reads: 'The 2 of May 1643 ye Crosse in Cheapside was pulled downe, a Troope of Horse & 2 Companies of foote wayted to garde it & at ye fall of ye tope Crosse drommes beat trumpets blew & multitudes of Capes wayre throwne in ye Ayre, & a great shoute of People with joy, ye 2 of May the Almanake. sayeth, was ye invention of the Crosse, & 6 day at night was the

Leaden Popes burnt, in the place where it stood with ringinge of Bells, & a greate Acclamation & no hurt done in all these actions.' A few days later, the Book of Sports was burnt by the hangman on the spot where the cross had stood. British Library, London

A Plan of the City and Environs of London, as Fortified by Order of Parliament, in the Years 1642 & 1643; engraving from a late edition of William Maitland's *History of London*. British Museum, London

68 Detail of two pages of engravings from John Cruso's *Militarie Instructions for the Cavallrie*, 1632. British Library, London

English cavalry armour, first half of the seventeenth century. Victoria and Albert Museum, London

69 Prince Rupert; detail of an oil painting by William Dobson showing him with Colonel William Murray and Colonel John Russell, *c.* 1644. Private collection

71 Sir John Byron, later first Baron Byron; detail of an oil painting by William Dobson, probably painted *c.* 1644. Collection of Lieutenant-Colonel J. Leicester-Warren

72 View of the site of the battle of Edgehill, Warwickshire. *Photo The Leamington Courier*

73 Note on the battle of Edgehill by Sir Bernard de Gomme; manuscript, 1642. The Royal Library, Windsor. By gracious permission of Her Majesty the Queen

Reverse of a medal distributed among the Royalist forces after the battle of Edgehill, showing Charles, Prince of Wales, on horseback; by Thomas Rawlins, 1642. British Museum, London

Pikemen at the battle of Edgehill; detail of the engraved title-page of *Mercurius Rusticus. The Countrys Complaint Recounting the sad Events of the late unparalleld Rebellion*, 1685. British Museum, London

74 Page from a Royalist drill book entitled *The young Artillery man*. Reproduced from *Cropredy*

Bridge, 1644 by Dr Margaret Toynbee and Brigadier Peter Young, by kind permission of the publishers, The Roundwood Press (Publishers) Ltd

75 A musketeer; woodcut, first half of the seventeenth century

Carved wood figure of an infantryman, on the staircase of Cromwell House, Highgate, London, *c.* 1638. Montfort Missionary Society. *Photo Eileen Tweedy*

A commission for raising troops signed by Ferdinando, second Baron Fairfax, 3 October 1643. Nottingham Castle Museum

77 Windsor Castle, Berkshire; etching by Wenceslaus Hollar. British Museum, London

78 Prince Rupert; woodcut from *The Bloody Prince, Or a Declaration of the most cruell Practices of Prince Rupert and the rest of the Cavaliers, in fighting against God and the true members of His Church*, 22 April 1643. British Library, London

79 Standard of Sir William Waller; from an eighteenth-century edition of the Earl of Clarendon's *History of the Great Rebellion*. British Library, London

80 Henrietta Maria landing at Bridlington, Yorkshire, in 1643; contemporary engraving. National Army Museum, London

Lichfield Cathedral, Staffordshire, from the north-west

82 Medal struck to commemorate the surrender of Bristol, 1643. British Museum, London. *Photo Ray Gardner*

83 Sir Thomas Fairfax, later third Baron Fairfax; detail of an oil painting attributed to Edward Bower. By courtesy of The Earl Spencer

84 Sir Edward Massey at the time of the civil war; detail of an oil painting by Sir Peter Lely. The National Gallery of Canada, Ottawa

Lucius Cary, first Viscount Falkland; mezzotint by Charles Turner after a contemporary painting by Cornelius Johnson. British Museum, London

85 Map showing the area between Gloucester and Reading covered by the troops of the King and of the Earl of Essex in September 1643. Drawn by John Woodcock, after S. R. Gardiner, *History of the Great Civil War*

88 *A Solemn League and Covenant,* 1643; etching by Wenceslaus Hollar. British Museum, London

89 Interior of St Margaret's Church, Westminster, London. *Photo The Warburg Institute*

90 James Graham, first Marquis of Montrose; oil painting after William Dobson. Collection of the Duke of Montrose. *Photo National Galleries of Scotland*

James Butler, Marquis and first Duke of Ormonde; oil painting after Sir Peter Lely, *c.* 1665. National Portrait Gallery, London

91 Engraving of a painted glass window in the church at Farndon, Cheshire, 'containing portraits of Cheshire Gentlemen who attended King Charles I at the Siege of Chester'; after a drawing by the Very Rev. Hugh Cholmondeley, Dean of Chester. The window, put up after the Restoration, still exists, though in somewhat damaged condition. Grosvenor Museum, Chester

92 View and plan of Hull, Yorkshire; etching by Wenceslaus Hollar. British Museum, London

93 Charlotte de la Trémoille, Countess of Derby; oil painting by an unknown artist, *c.* 1657. National Portrait Gallery, London

95 View of Newark, Nottinghamshire, 'from Hawton way'; etching by Wenceslaus Hollar, 1676. British Museum, London

96–7 View of York from the south; engraving by William Lodge, 1678. British Library, London

98 Hanwell Castle, Oxfordshire. *Photo Gordon Norwood,* reproduced from *Cropredy Bridge, 1644* by Dr Margaret Toynbee and Brigadier Peter Young, by kind permission of the publishers, The

Roundwood Press (Publishers) Ltd

99 Civil war armour and medieval brass lectern in Cropredy Church, Oxfordshire. *Photo Frank Smallpage*

101 Soldiers marching; woodcut from a broadsheet entitled *Jockies Lamentation* (on the defeat of the Scots at the battle of Dunbar), 1650. British Library, London

102 Alexander Leslie, first Earl of Leven; oil painting by an unknown artist. Scottish National Portrait Gallery, Edinburgh

Detail of a broadsheet printing a letter from Sir James Lumsden reporting on the battle of Marston Moor, Yorkshire, published in Edinburgh in 1644. Reproduced by courtesy of the Trustees of the National Library of Scotland, Edinburgh

102–3 Plan of the battle of Marston Moor by Sir Bernard de Gomme; pen and wash, 1644. MS. Add. 16370, f. 64. British Library, London

105 Oliver Cromwell; unfinished miniature by Samuel Cooper, probably painted *c.* 1650. Collection of the Duke of Buccleuch and Queensberry

107 Plan showing the fortifications of Plymouth, Devon, and the Royalist siege-works in 1643; etching by Wenceslaus Hollar. British Museum, London

108 Shaw House, near Newbury, Berkshire. *Photo The British Tourist Authority*

109 The gatehouse of Donnington Castle, Berkshire. *Photo National Monuments Record*

111 Execution of William Laud; engraving from a broadsheet entitled *A Prognostication upon W. Laud,* 10 January 1645. British Library, London

113 Oliver Cromwell; detail of an oil painting based on Robert Walker's portrait of *c.* 1649, made for Queen Christina of Sweden. Nationalmuseum, Stockholm. *Photo Svenska Porträttarkivet, Stockholm*

Edward Montagu, second Earl of Manchester; detail of an oil paint-

ing by Sir Peter Lely, 1661–65. National Portrait Gallery, London

114 Title-page of *The Souldiers Catechisme,* London, 1644. Trustees of the London Museum, on loan to the Cromwell Museum, Huntingdon

116 Sir Thomas Fairfax presiding over the Council of the Army, 1647

117 Uniform of a cavalry trooper of the New Model Army, from Littlecote House, Wiltshire. Tower of London Armouries. *Photo Crown copyright, reproduced with the permission of the Controller of Her Majesty's Stationery Office*

118 Charles II when Prince of Wales, with a page; oil painting by William Dobson, probably painted in 1643. Scottish National Portrait Gallery, Edinburgh. *Photo National Galleries of Scotland*

119 A Royalist field-camp; detail of an etching by Wenceslaus Hollar. British Museum, London

120 Henry Ireton; miniature by Samuel Cooper, 1649. Reproduced by permission of the Syndics of the Fitzwilliam Museum, Cambridge

Sir Marmaduke Langdale, first Baron Langdale of Holme; mezzotint after a contemporary portrait, 1774. British Museum, London

121 Map of the campaign of Naseby, Leicestershire, 1645. Drawn by John Woodcock, after S. R. Gardiner, *History of the Great Civil War*

122–3 The battle of Naseby; engraving by Streeter from Joshua Sprigge's *Anglia Rediviva,* London, 1647. British Library, London

125 George Goring, Baron Goring; detail of an oil painting showing Goring with the Earl of Newport, after Sir Anthony van Dyck, *c.* 1635–40. National Portrait Gallery, London

127 Basing House, Hampshire, under siege in 1645 or before; contemporary engraving. Victoria and Albert Museum, London. *Photo John Webb (Brompton Studio)*

Wenceslaus Hollar; etched by himself after a portrait painted by

Johannes Meyssens when Hollar was abroad in 1645–52. British Museum, London

Inigo Jones; drawing by Sir Anthony van Dyck (d. 1641). Devonshire Collection, Chatsworth. Reproduced by Permission of the Trustees of the Chatsworth Settlement

Ruins of Basing House. *Photo the Hants Field Club*

128–9 View of Chester from the River Dee, with the castle on the left; pen and wash drawing by Francis Place, 1699. Victoria and Albert Museum, London

130 Air view of the Queen's Sconce, Newark, Nottinghamshire. *Photo the Committee for Aerial Photography, University of Cambridge*

Detail of a plan of the siege of Newark in 1646; engraving by Percival Lovell. British Library, London

131 Set of three woodcuts showing beggars, mid-seventeenth century

132 Crown minted in Oxford during the siege, *c.* 1646. British Museum, London. *Photo Ray Gardner*

William Dobson; oil painting after a self-portrait, *c.* 1642–46. National Portrait Gallery, London

132–3 Oxford in 1644. The original drawing is in reverse; it is likely that it was prepared for an engraving, in which the design would have appeared right-way-round. The lettering was subsequently added, but not in reverse (so that in our reproduction it is reversed). North is at the bottom. Within the outer fortifications the town is partially surrounded by its own medieval walls, at the right-hand (eastern) end of which is the castle. At the opposite end of town Magdalen College stands outside the walls, next to the bridge over the Cherwell. Christ Church College is at the centre, labelled T, with Merton near by (X). MS. Wood 376 B, f. 30. By courtesy of the Curators of the Bodleian Library, Oxford

134 Corfe Castle, Dorset. *Photo Edwin Smith*

135 'The English-Irish Soldier'; woodcut from a broadsheet (suggesting that the soldiers sent by the King to suppress the Irish revolt in 1641–42 would be better at plundering than fighting), 1642. British Library, London

136 William Cavendish, Earl, Marquis and later first Duke of Newcastle, on horseback before Bolsover Castle, Derbyshire; engraving by A. Diepenbeke from Newcastle's *Méthode Nouvelle*, 1658. British Library, London

138 Engraved title-page of *Mercurius Rusticus. The Countrys Complaint Recounting the sad Events of the late unparalleld Rebellion,* 1685. British Museum, London

139 Iconoclastic soldiers in Yorkshire; etching by Wenceslaus Hollar from John Vicars' *Sight of the Transactions of these latter yeares,* London, 1646. British Library, London

140 *Five Orders and Ordinance Of Parliament, For payment of Soldiers,* 11–15 June 1647. British Library, London

141 The Sun Inn and near-by houses in Saffron Walden, Essex. *Photo The British Tourist Authority*

142 Title-page of *The Declaration and Standard of the Levellers of England,* 23 April 1649. *Photo Radio Times Hulton Picture Library*

143 John Lilburne standing trial at the Guildhall, London, 1649; detail of a contemporary engraving. British Museum, London

146 Title-page of a pamphlet including *His Majesties Demands to Collonel Hammond,* 1648. British Library, London

147 Charles I imprisoned in Carisbrooke Castle, Isle of Wight; woodcut from the title-page of *An Ould Ship called an Exhortation To continue all Subjects in their due Obedience, or the reward of a faithfull Subject to his Prince,* 1648. British Library, London

Letter from Charles I to his chambermaid, Mary, written at Carisbrooke Castle, 31 January 1648. MS. Add. 7311, f. 2r. Cambridge University Library

148 *A Harmany of Healths,* beginning of a Royalist song-sheet published in London. The Manchester Public Libraries

149 Pembroke Castle. *Photo The British Tourist Authority*

150 John Lambert; detail of an oil painting after Robert Walker. National Portrait Gallery, London

151 Obverse and reverse of a unique gold twenty-shilling piece struck at Pontefract Castle, Yorkshire, during the siege, and dating from February or March 1649. British Museum, London

152 The Old Siege House, Colchester, Essex. *Photo The British Tourist Authority*

153 Detail of a plan showing the siege of Colchester, 1648; contemporary engraving. British Museum, London

155 Engraved title-page of *The Loyall Sacrifice,* showing the execution of Sir Charles Lucas and Sir George Lisle at Colchester, 1648. British Museum, London

156 Title-page of *A Declaration for Peace from the Kings most Excellent Majesty,* London, 1648. British Library, London

157 Charles I at his trial; oil painting by Edward Bower, 1649. By gracious permission of Her Majesty Queen Elizabeth, the Queen Mother

158 Title-page of John Milton's *The Tenure of Kings and Magistrates,* London, 1649. British Library, London

158–9 Commemorative picture of the execution of Charles I; oil painting by the Flemish artist Weesop, 1649. The medallion above left shows Charles I. The executioner holding the King's head, in the medallion at the upper right, has the features of Sir Thomas Fairfax (compare the portrait, p. 83): according to a rumour circulating abroad, it was Fairfax himself who had beheaded the King. Below left, the King is led to his execution; below right, people rush to dip their handkerchiefs in the blood of the 'martyred' King. Collection of Lord Primrose, on loan to the Scottish National Portrait Gallery, Edinburgh. *Photo National Galleries of Scotland*

INDEX

Numbers in *italic* type refer to pages on which illustrations appear